ABOUT THE AUTHOR

Dr Elizabeth Tierney, author of *Show Time! A Guide to Making Effective Presentations*, is currently Process Consultant to the Marketing Development Programme in the Graduate School of Business at University College Dublin and a lecturer in the Business Administration Department. She speaks, consults and trains in such areas as Presentation Skills, Trainer Training, Report Writing, Business Ethics and Humanities for Leadership. During her career in the United States, Dr Tierney was both a personnel recruiter and a director of personnel.

SELLING YOURSELF

A Practical Guide to Job Hunting

Elizabeth P. Tierney

Oak Tree Press

Dublin

Oak Tree Press
Merrion Building
Lower Merrion Street
Dublin 2

A catalogue record for this book
is available from the British Library.

ISBN 1-872853-55-2

2 4 6 8 10 9 7 5 3

Printed in Ireland by
Colour Books, Ltd., Dublin.

CONTENTS

Chapter 1

GETTING STARTED

"When she asked me to list my weaknesses, no problem. I rattled off that I like to sleep in in the mornings, tend to put things off a bit, and, well, how can I put it? I am not all that organised. But when she asked me to list my strengths, I hadn't a clue what to say. I went blank. Couldn't come up with one. Oh, well. What happened with you, Suzanne? How did your interview go? What were you asked?"

"Thank goodness, I wasn't asked about my strengths and weaknesses, Bren! But I got stuck, too, when my interviewer asked why I was applying. I told him point blank that I just needed a job, that this one sounded great, 'cause I wanted to do some travelling before I got married."

Brendan and Suzanne took a break from their postmortem of the morning's events and sipped their coffee at a quiet table in Bewley's. After further exchanges about their respective job interviews and in spite of some nagging doubts, both were feeling surprisingly confident, given the stress of the morning.

"Did he say when he was calling you back?" Brendan asked finally.

"Don't know," said Suzanne, shrugging her shoulders. "He did say that there were a lot of applicants and that he was interviewing quite a few, so he'd be in touch. Anyway, at least *we* got interviews. I was talking to Clare and John the other day. They're not feeling great. Neither one has had any luck at all. They've been sending out their CVs and nothing is happening. Not a single bite."

"Hey, I forgot to tell you that I met Simon last week," said Brendan. "He's feeling down, too. Says that there are no jobs out there, nothing in the papers."

Based on these snippets of conversation, it is difficult to know what will develop on the job front for each of the five, but at the moment it is certainly not sounding good for any of them. Simon is waiting for a job to be advertised in the newspaper. Clare and John cannot seem to get their feet in the door. Despite the fact that Brendan and Suzanne made it to first-round interviews, based on the answers we overheard, don't put money on their being invited back for a second. When asked, Brendan could think only of his flaws and none of his attributes. Suzanne appears to have told the interviewer that she'd take anything and was somewhat casual about why she wanted the job, never indicating what she could offer the company. Neither Brendan's nor Suzanne's responses are good ones.

What should all five be doing instead to increase their odds of being hired?

This book is written to answer that question, to help them, or you, or anyone who is in the market for a job. That includes school leavers, university graduates, career changers or anyone re-entering the labour market or looking for an internal promotion or transfer. Most of us no longer stay in one job for life, so we will go through the job-hunting process many times, and we will need to use those same skills again and again.

Although, as Suzanne suggested, luck and good fortune — being in the right place at the right time — can have a lot to do with successful job hunting, you also need to rely on your own efforts. There *are* jobs out there. To land the job that's right for you takes more than a good horoscope or insightful palm reading, however. Quite simply, you must understand the process and know how to sell yourself.

Do you know anyone who earns a living in sales? Talk to that person. Find out what it takes to sell. You will learn that it takes intelligence, hard work, motivation and persistence. Successful salespeople must have a thorough knowledge of what they have to offer prospective buyers. They also know the market and the competition. Successful salespeople face rejections and know not only how to accept them but how to refocus and redouble their energies. Successful salespeople don't lose sight of their objectives. The same should be true for people in the job market. You need to be smart, to work hard and to dig your heels in despite the rejections. You need to know what you have to offer; you need to know the market, that is, who is hiring whom and why, and you need to believe that, with determination and persistence, you will ultimately, despite setbacks, prevail. You will be hired.

To clarify how job hunting and selling are similar, let's use some analogies. Think for a moment about an ad campaign that you have seen, any campaign, be it for soup or soap. The images, the copy, or the voice-over may encourage you to consider buying the product because of its unique qualities: the soup may be tasty, the soap kind to your skin. Another example: you might decide to buy one particular item rather than another because a shop assistant convinces you that one of the two products you are considering may enhance your life, save you money or ease some burden. Because you prefer the qualities that one brand has over another, you buy *it* instead of the other. In the same way, you need to convince or persuade the job interviewer to select you over others.

Imagine another scenario: you want to persuade some friends to go with you to see a particular film. What's your strategy? Well, what you do *not* do is underline the flaws of the movie, by saying that the story is "boring", the acting "desperate" and the cinematography "poor". What you probably do instead is encourage them to go by highlighting the good aspects, perhaps by citing the one actor who is great, the remarkable ending and the brilliant soundtrack. In each case — be it the ad campaign, the sales assistant recommending that you buy one brand over another or you convincing friends to go to a particular film — you or someone else is persuading, selling, and by doing so, highlighting those aspects that will make you or someone else want to taste, wash, buy or go to the cinema.

Some experienced salespeople use an acronym to capture the elements of selling: AIDA. A is for attention, I for interest, D for desire and A for action. When a salesperson wants to sell a product, he or she remembers that the first step in the process is to get the (A) attention of the prospective buyers. The second step is to (I) interest the buyers in the benefits of the product so much so that they (D) desire it. Then it is essential to get the buyers to (A), to act on that desire by placing an order or making a purchase. The acronym applies to you, too, in your campaign to sell yourself. You want to attract the attention of prospective employers. You want them to be so interested in what you can bring to the firm that they want to have you on board. They act, by making you an offer. Remember AIDA. Use the elements of that technique to sell yourself.

Now, Brendan, Suzanne, Clare, John and Simon are certainly not soup, nor are they soap. Neither are you. They and you are unique individuals. But when you are looking for a job, you must bear in mind the sales techniques which are used to encourage you to buy a product or a concept. You must bear in mind the strategy you employ to motivate others to do something: to go to a film, to read a book, to take a trip, to lend the car, to clean their rooms. The essence of the job hunt is to persuade others to consider you as a potential employee. To do that, you sell yourself.

In addition to reminding you that you must sell yourself, the book will assist you in understanding what's involved in the overall process of job hunting. Begin by analysing yourself and by believing in the quality of what you have to offer. Then, learn about the market and consider more proactive ways of opening doors. Don't be like poor Simon, who sits around waiting for the perfect ad to appear magically one day in the newspaper and, in the meantime, moans that there are no jobs out there.

Clare and John and you — whether you're a recent graduate seeking your first serious job or someone re-entering the labour market — are going to have to write effective CVs and covering letters, if you expect to get interviews. You also must become more comfortable with the interview process itself, so that, unlike Brendan, you can emphasise your strengths rather than list your weaknesses, or unlike Suzanne, you can turn your answers around and understand the importance of considering the company's perspective, thus improving

your chances of being called back for a second interview. You will also need to think about your referees
and what to do if an offer of a position is made.

What Do You Need?

To get started, you'll need a few bits and pieces, a few
tools. First, you should make a few purchases: a pen, a
refill pad or two, good quality white or off-white writing paper and envelopes, and a diary. If you don't have
access to a typewriter or word processor, find a friend
who does. There are some other things which you won't
be able to purchase but which you will nevertheless
need to acquire: patience, determination and a firm conviction that you have something valuable to offer an
employer. Believing in yourself is the hard bit. That's
why Brendan's ability to reel off weaknesses is not sur-
prising. If asked to expand on his answer, he probably
could have come up with a few more faults: "difficulty
saying no", "leaving things to the last minute", "not
following through". Most of us are very good at putting
ourselves down and about telling other people what is
wrong with us. Our faults seem endless: we're too fat,
too thin, too stupid, no good at maths, terrible at
spelling, can't sing, can't dance, can't cook, can't play
snooker.

Intellectually we may accept the notion that it is
acceptable to tell the good points about soup or soap or
films. However, if we have the ego to admit to having
good or useful qualities, we think it is somehow im-
modest and downright arrogant to say it aloud and,
worse yet, to someone else. But, if you don't learn to
verbalise what your talents are, you are requiring
potential employers to be archaeologists and to dig to

uncover your hidden abilities. Interviewers may not have the time or the interest to unearth your hidden treasures. If you want to sell yourself to a prospective employer, you will need to get past the fear of being struck by a lightning bolt if you say something nice about yourself.

What Have You Got to Offer?

It's pointless applying for a position until you know what you have to sell to a prospective employer. You have to ask yourself: What do I want to do? What do I have to offer the company? At this stage it's time to reflect rather than act, so no skipping forward to the CV chapter.

Let's begin with some self-analysis. This process of reflection is an opportunity for you to take an intensive look at yourself, to identify the special talents, abilities, skills and/or knowledge that you have to offer, as well as to focus on the kind of work that you prefer to do. You may think this is a silly waste of time. "I know myself well already," you say. But it can't hurt to take an additional hard look at yourself. Furthermore, much of this thinking will enable you to identify the precise words that you can incorporate into your CV, your covering letter or your answers to questions during an interview.

If you are someone who is not sure about what you want to do or what abilities you have, then this self-audit is a useful exercise for eliminating certain kinds of jobs from your consideration and for focusing on others. For example, if you're claustrophobic, maybe a job as a lift operator or a submarine commander is out. If you don't like pressure, then telesales or a job in the stock-

market may have to go. If you enjoy people, being a
shepherd may not be for you. Although these are ex-
treme examples, what you like and dislike, need or
thrive on will affect your enthusiasm or suitability for
positions. And you can be sure that your enthusiasm or
lack of it will be detected by an interviewer.

Let's start your audit by using a few sheets of your
refill pad. Head a few pages "Education", several more
"Work", and three or four more pages "Leisure" or
"Social".

Then make three columns on each page. The first
column on the work page should say "Jobs", the next
column should have a plus sign at the top and the third a
minus sign. The first page, therefore, may look like this:

WORK

Job(s)	+	−

Make three similar columns on the education pages
and on the social ones. However, instead of the word
"jobs" under "Education", you might list "courses", and
under "Social" your first heading might be "activities".

Now find a quiet place where you can concentrate,
and then start with your work experience. In the first
column list every job you have ever had. You may need
more than one page. "Every job" includes those at
weekends, nights, summers, part-time, full-time. Omit

nothing: bartending, **babysitting**, flight attending, shoe-selling, shelf-stocking, household managing, car washing, teaching. Now, next to each job, in the positive (+) column write phrases or words that capture a positive side of the job. Try to use as many verbs as you can — action words. For example, the pluses might be handling accounts, organising the family, handling a difficult customer, travelling, being responsible, helping someone learn.

Once you've done that, fill in the column on the negative side (–) for each of the positions that you held. To do so, recall what you disliked about the job, what you dreaded. Was it the routine? The difficult customers? The pressure? The management's attitude? The page may now look something like this:

WORK

Job(s)	+	–
Sales Assistant	working with people making friends the kinds of products the customers	the hours the waiting keeping inventory wrapping packages the boss never noticed me
Receptionist	people the phone diversity the fast pace handling problems	no growth having to do the filing not enough responsibility

You'll find that as you think back you'll be reminded of situations that are long forgotten. As those memories surface, jot down notes: the time you were asked to handle a particular project or attend a meeting or when you organised a special event. Recall the evening that you babysat and couldn't get the children to sleep or the time you tended bar and hefted cases all night. Write it down!

Then follow the same procedure with the page headed "Education". Next to each course or class again write down words or phrases which reflect both positive and negative experiences that you have had. Don't limit your list to first, second and third level. Don't forget to include any special courses that you may have taken: key-boarding, banking, language, swimming or driving. Next to each one indicate the pluses and minuses, in other words, the positive and negative aspects of each experience. For example, the analysis in maths may have been great, the rote memory demanded in history was not; the independent research you did was a plus, the group work was not, perhaps because you felt frustrated.

Under the plus column, jot down what you were praised for by your teachers. Thoughtfulness? Creativity? Conscientious behaviour? Assuming responsibility? Also include any special recognition you earned. Did you get an award or a prize? As you remember your classes, think about when your classmates may have turned to you for help or advice. Was it your knowledge of subject matter? Your patience? Your ability to communicate? Did you have good notes? Did you understand trigonometry or the meaning of *Lord of the Flies*? Did you write well? Have a good memory? Get on with the teachers? And when did you turn to others to seek help? Or didn't you? The education page might begin to look like this:

EDUCATION

Courses/classes	+	−
Secondary	algebra — pressure problem solving working independently having responsibility history — reading English teacher — encouraging	routine boring classes confusing directions regimentation pressure of exams having to memorise no creativity!
Keyboard Course	developing a skill friends	practising repetition

Now follow the same process on your next page, "Leisure". List in the left column all the activities that you have undertaken in your spare time. What are the pluses? What do you enjoy in your leisure time? What are the minuses? What do you least enjoy? Watching TV? Playing sports? Which sports? Why? Listening to music? Playing an instrument? Do you read or do you not like to? Do you enjoy walking? Cycling? Chatting with friends? Going to the pub? Being on your own? Going to the theatre? Playing computer games? Writing poetry? Fishing? Collecting tropical fish? And what are the pluses and the minuses about each one?

LEISURE

Activities	+	−
Tennis	competition being outside friends	waiting for a court losing

Your thoughts are so important that it's worth taking
several days to keep adding recollections to each page.
Once you have, it's time to think about those experiences and the pluses and minuses of each of them *and* to
do so from a business perspective.

What's a business perspective? What has playing
tennis or enjoying Clint Eastwood movies or collecting
stamps or babysitting got to do with business? The
answer is lots! Business is about people working alone
or in groups to achieve an objective. So is school. So
are all your jobs. So is your leisure time.

Put your notes aside for the moment and ask yourself
what people do in business. Think about how business
people spend their days. For example, shopkeepers,
managers, bus drivers may have to plan, attend meetings, follow schedules, make decisions, meet deadlines,
work with different people, encounter problems, work
in groups, work on their own, write reports, arrange
meetings, supervise others, delegate, telephone, fax,
read, speak, analyse, solve problems, interview.

So, look at your three lists. Look at the words you
used to describe the positive or negative experiences.
Do you begin to see business behaviours? Stacking
shelves may be about working under pressure, or following directions or keeping inventory. Being in the
school play may be about working for someone or about
attending to details. Running a household or raising children involves scheduling, communicating, organising,
budgeting, motivating, to name a few. Think of how all
that transfers to business. Also look at what was a plus
or preference for you. Look at what was a negative,
what you disliked. Think in terms of transferring all
those abilities, skills and talents from school, leisure and,
of course, working life to the world of business.

Furthermore, analyse your preferences in business terms and see if you can see any patterns emerging. For example, if you have always enjoyed playing sports, think of what skills, talents, or attributes are involved in that activity. Are you competitive? A team player? Do you prefer the practice sessions or the match? Is it the camaraderie that you enjoy? The risk? The leadership? The winning? The outdoors? The pace?

If, on the other hand, you prefer *watching* sports, is it the analysis that you like? The problem-solving? The comparative statistics? The safety? The lack of responsibility? Suppose under "Social" you wrote that you like to read. Think about why you do and what you choose to read, what you enjoy. Do you read to escape? Is it the use of the imagination that attracts you? The creativity? The analysis? The use of words? The hard facts? The acquisition and application of new knowledge?

Analyse what happened in school. Did you enjoy history more than maths? Why? Were these situations when you were the leader? The follower? Both? Which role did you prefer? Did you work well under pressure? Were you sensitive to the politics? Were you organised? Did you recommend new ideas? Did you help others?

As you review all the plus and minus columns, you may notice emerging in those three aspects of your life skills, talents or preferences which are applicable to business. For example, you may recognise that you enjoy working and playing under pressure or you may not. You may prefer meeting new people or you may not. You may prefer focusing on one item at a time or you may not. You may like learning or you may not. You may enjoy technology or you may not. You may like to motivate or you may not. You may like to work on your own or you may not.

There are sophisticated psychological tests you could take to learn more about your own preferences, but the act of self-reflection suggested here should assist you in recognising talents that you have and can bring to an organisation. This self-analysis will aid you in identifying talents or skills that you may have taken for granted. In fact, if you are in the job hunt now, you may not be articulating those abilities in your letters, on your CVs or in your interviews. To date, you may be indicating that you have six months' experience as a waitress in a restaurant in Martha's Vineyard or five years' working as an accounts clerk in a bank in Galway or that you have a particular certificate, award, diploma or degree to offer. But what you may not be indicating to a prospective employer is what was involved in those experiences, what skills you used or what you learned about people, technology, or handling situations or ideas.

Throughout your career you will be offering prospective employers direct hands-on experience. You will also be offering how you learn, how you behave, and how you deal with problems. In other words, you are offering YOU, the person, the unique whole person, the one who is spontaneous or thoughtful or cautious or smart or calculating or imaginative or funny. You are presenting someone who likes to organise, who likes to explain technical problems, someone who can motivate people or manage difficult ones, someone who is happier in a structured environment, or who prefers an unstructured one.

Now look at your notes again and identify your strengths, because that's what they are. Take another sheet of paper and make another list entitled "What I Do Well".

What I Do Well

- organise
- persuade people
- find creative solutions
- get on with people
- attend to detail

As you make this list, it is useful to think about your peers, as you did earlier. What do you do better than others? "More arrogance?" you ask. No, honesty. You know what you do better because of what you have seen or what people have told you. Your friends have said, "You are so good at organising ideas", or they have asked your advice about certain concerns. Your teachers or bosses may have complimented you. As you reflect, you will also become aware of what your colleagues, the competition, do better than you do. You may be better than they at having ideas. They may be better at implementing them. You may prefer taking time to think through a problem, rather than having to decide quickly. For example, Brendan may have got honours in maths, but he cannot stand up to speak in front of a group of people without going to pieces. Suzanne may have a great sense of humour, but she prefers to lead rather than to follow. John is shy, but he solves problems quickly.

For those of you who are still unsure of what you want to do, reflect on your talents and preferences as you read the classified ads and job descriptions. Given what you know about yourself, ask yourself which jobs in the list do not interest you. Forget the money, disregard the benefits, and read the qualifications, even if you don't have the specialised knowledge called for.

Would you want to be a guard, a teacher, a plant supervisor, a bank teller, a receptionist, an accounts clerk, a creative director, a salesperson, a proofreader? Read what the company is looking for. Think about how people in these jobs might spend their days. Then compare what they do with what you like or dislike doing, what you are good at and what you are not good at. Of course, if you cannot imagine what a proofreader does, find one and ask about the job or do some reading on the subject.

Don't eliminate being a pilot because currently you don't have the technical know-how. Your willingness and interest in learning is critical. Remember, learning is an important point. No matter what position you have, or will have, you will have to learn something new. It's a cliché, but the world is changing quickly as is the work environment. Look back at your "What I Do Well" list and check to see what you wrote about learning. Did you write anything? If not, maybe you should. By the way, read your list of strengths out loud. Hear yourself saying them. Those are some of your selling points, and they should come off your pen or tongue with ease!

After you have done the self-analysis, don't belittle what you discover about yourself. Don't hide your "What I Do Well" list. Admit to yourself that an organisation will benefit from your abilities: your energy, your unflappability under pressure, your loyalty, your empathy, your skill with computers, your insight into people, your organising ability, your positive outlook, your willingness to learn, your flexibility, your charm, your patience, your "sticktoitivity" in adversity, your ability to conceptualise, your ability to attend to details. Based on your personal audit you know what your preferences are and what you do well. Therefore, you should also accept the fact that you will be frustrated, bored or unhappy in the wrong position.

Handling Rejection

As pleased as you should be by what you have to offer and being aware that not every job is for you, remember also that not every company is going to need or want your unique combination of talents. A hi-tech organisation may not need a calligrapher, a car repair shop may not need a skilled researcher. Think, too, about the different organisations with which you have been associated, and remember that each has its own working style and culture. Dramsoc may have been go-go-go, while the chess club couldn't organise a meeting. Your secondary school may have been strict and regulated, while your primary school was open and friendly.

In other words, what you are offering may not be what works or is appropriate for a particular company. You may have the knowledge or the skills being sought, but the organisation may be looking for an employee who enjoys repetition or for whom security is important. You, on the other hand, may thrive on challenge and change. In the short term you may be delighted to have a job, but in the longer term, you wouldn't be, and the company wouldn't be either. In hiring terms, you and the company are not a good match. So, like any good salesperson, you had better be prepared for rejection.

Therefore, when you begin the job hunt armed with your paper and pencils and conviction and determination, it would be advisable to find a human ally — a

family member, colleague, loved one, friend, instructor
— to whom you can turn for support when the rejection
comes. And it will come. Job hunting is tough. It hurts.
At different stages in the process you will be told "no".
As in John's case, your CV may not contain what the
company is looking for; the talents and skills you list
may not be exactly what the company needs. Another
candidate, perhaps, will offer something that you can't.
Or after the interviews, someone else will fit the organisation better. Your ally is there to remind you that you
are talented.

You should also take out the "What I Do Well" list
and reread it. Try to separate that sense of rejection
from your sense of self-worth, difficult as that may be to
do. What the company is saying when it doesn't hire
you is that your combination of qualities or talents is not
what they need at this time. You may interpret that to
mean that you as a person are worthless. Remember,
however, that you are being rejected as a candidate for a
specific position in a certain organisation. You are not
being rejected as a human being. By the way, check that
"What I Do Well" list. Does it include "good loser"?

Face it, we have all experienced rejection. We have
all come in second or third or last — the part in the play
that went to someone else, the front seat of the car next
to Dad, the captain of the team, the present that you
wished for and that wasn't there on Christmas morning,
the argument about an in-law that you didn't win.
Someone else was picked to erase the board or was
elected class president. We have all lost on some
occasions; we have all experienced disappointments.

It's not as if these feelings are new. What matters is
your ability to bounce back from a loss. If you got
knocked to the canvas in the first round as boxer

Michael Carruth did in his first professional fight, could you redouble your efforts as he did to come back to win? Or would you give up? The challenge doesn't have to be a championship fight. It takes determination to master scales on the piano, to end a relationship and to risk establishing another one. There are times when you will be hurt, angry, frustrated and disappointed. Giving up is easy. So, do what you do to get out of the dumps. Rationalise, go for a run, take a walk, see a *Rocky* movie — talk to a friend, and then try again!

What is Going On Out There?

Armed with paper, pen, conviction and friend, knowing better what talents you have to offer — your selling points, your personal inventory — you now need to know what is going on in the market.

First, though, let's be clear: there *are* jobs out there. There really are. Despite high unemployment figures and disheartening news for job seekers, people are working, people are being hired, changing careers, retiring, entering the workforce or applying for positions within their own organisations and being promoted.

So how do you find out about all that activity? You learn about the market by reading: magazines, books, journals, newspapers. You learn by watching TV, by listening to the radio; you learn by talking to people. You need to become aware of what is going on generally in the marketplace. What are the latest trends? What is changing? What is the latest technology? Because we are living longer, what is happening in healthcare? What are the implications of a global economy, of more labour-saving appliances, of more women in the workforce, of people working from home? Is advertising undergoing changes? Is concern for the environment opening up new areas of employment?

In other words, get a feel for what is or is not changing in the workplace, and, therefore, what industries are hiring and which ones probably are not. Toxic waste disposal or telecommunications? Coal mining or geriatric medicine? Aviation or tourism? If you see an industry sector that appeals to you, focus on the specific organisations in it. Are those companies expanding? Merging? Relocating? Closing? Does a newspaper article suggest that a new product or service is being launched by a particular firm? Will the company need more people? In what area? Or is it too late?

In addition, as you do your homework by reading, talking and watching, you will also learn about job titles and about who got a promotion and about what specific company is adding staff. Find out whom they hire and what kind of qualifications they look for in a candidate. While you have been analysing yourself and the qualities that you have to sell, you are also analysing the market to look for prospective employers. Who is hiring whom? What kinds of industries are developing, and what kinds of skills, talents, abilities do they need? Perhaps you see that financial institutions are growing. "Finance isn't for me," you say, "I hate numbers." But don't be so hasty. Is finance all numbers? Isn't someone selling services? Doing some research? Supervising? Handling customers? Think carefully about the specific job duties before you rule out an entire industry.

Up to now you have been reflecting, making lists, analysing, questioning, listening and researching as well as practising saying nice things about yourself without being struck dumb. It's time to get down to a different kind of work. It's time to plan your campaign. Whether

you are a recent grad, a career changer, a mum return-
ing to the workforce, a successful businessperson who
wants to make a move, it's time to get your strategy in
order. It's fine to know who's hiring whom, but it's up
to you to let companies know what you have to offer
and that you are in the market for a job or a change of
jobs.

So, with your pages of refill pad filled in, your "What
I Do Well" list at hand, it's time to think about how you
are going to open doors, what you want to include in
your CV, what you want to highlight in your covering
letters, what to write on your applications and how to
prepare for interviews. Then, you will need to cope with
the "no" and have the determination to apply elsewhere.
Or, hopefully, happily to negotiate an offer and think
about gracefully leaving your current employer. With
your selling points in mind, it's time to work on getting
the employers' attention and interest.

Chapter 2

OPENING DOORS

So how do you find the job openings? How do you let prospective employers know that you are available and eager to work? As we said earlier, employers cannot hire you unless they know that you are out there. How do you let it be known that you are in the market? What are some of the approaches that you can use to open doors?

Some methods are more passive than others. Simon, as we know, reads through the job ads and will act only if he sees an interesting position advertised. Waiting for the ads is essentially a passive approach, as is watching for job postings on bulletin boards. Networking and writing to companies "on spec" require more initiative and entrepreneurial spirit than Simon has shown to date. Because he's being passive rather than active, he's limiting his opportunities. There's nothing wrong with following up a printed lead; do it, by all means. But Simon is depending solely on others. He's not doing all that he might to put himself forward as a candidate for positions or, for that matter, to have a position created for him. And the latter can happen, particularly if the decision-makers in an organisation are impressed with the background, capabilities, ingenuity and entre-preneurial spirit of a candidate.

Let's look at a number of ways in which you can either find out what is going on in the job market or introduce yourself as a viable candidate for positions.

Checking Classified Advertisements

Like Simon, most of us read the job vacancies section of a newspaper, magazine and/or professional journal as the first step toward learning which companies are looking for what kinds of candidates. Reading ads is the easiest approach. All you have to do is to buy the periodicals, or to go to a library or coffee shop which has them, and read through the columns of ads. The process is even easier when the ads are alphabetical. You see a position advertised or you do not. If you don't see something intriguing, you wait for the next edition. Even if you do notice an opening, you read next week's or next month's issue to see what else there is. You read the ads and decide once again that there is or is not a position suitable for you. Until you find an ad worth responding to, you become a regular reader of job vacancy ads, be it a two-line ad or one that takes up an entire quarter page.

Because scanning the ads is the easiest method of job hunting, it should come as no surprise to you that many other people are doing exactly what you are doing. If they decide actually to apply too, you can imagine what the competition must be like for each position. Picture the piles of CVs landing on recruiters' desks, and you will understand why you should consider using other methods as well as ad scanning.

Regardless of whether or not studying ads is a popular approach, what do you do if you see a job that looks interesting and for which you believe you are suited? First of all, photocopy the ad, write the date and source — for example, 12/9/199x, *The Irish Times* — or clip the ad out and save it for future reference. Having a copy of the ad is important because you will want to refer to it when you draft your covering letter. Understand that someone in the organisation has taken time to write a description of the position and to identify the essential qualifications. So, when you apply, pay close attention to that description and those qualifications. No company is interested in receiving hundreds of CVs and letters from prospective candidates who don't qualify. In short, be sure that you are suited for the position.

As you know, many ads give not only the job title but also list specific requirements such as "two years' experience in the field", "knowledge of French", "high energy", etc. What follows may sound contradictory, but although your abilities and experience should match the requirements, it is important not to eliminate yourself from applying because you don't *precisely* meet the specifications. For example, you may be three months short of the required two years' experience, or the ad may indicate "knowledge of French", not "fluency in French". In this instance, therefore, if you have a reading knowledge of French but cannot speak it, consider applying, *if* you also have the other requirements.

Don't assume that everyone else reading the ad will be a perfect match either. But again remember that you don't want to waste the company's time. If the organisation is calling for two years' experience working in the Middle East and you've never even left town, don't apply. However, if in doubt, let them decide. The managers or recruiters will be making their own decisions about which applicants to call for interviews based on the other letters and CVs that they receive, not just on yours. For example, if the firm wants fluent French but no candidate has it, the recruiters may readvertise or decide to consider someone who has studied it and who is prepared to take courses. Therefore, you might be still in the running. Remember, if the job is important to you, you can always indicate a willingness to learn in those areas in which you are deficient.

Answering an Ad

Let's now apply for a job that you have seen advertised and which interests you. Read the ad carefully and do exactly what the instructions tell you to do. It may be obvious to say that, but people often get knocked out of the running for positions because they didn't do what they were instructed to do in the ad.

For example, if the ad states, "phone for an application", then phone for an application. If it states, "send a letter of interest and CV to Personnel at Tremendo, plc", then do so. If it states, "submit your paperwork by 5 March", then get it in by 5 March, not the 6th, the 12th or the 15th. Every job requires you to follow instructions of some kind, so part of the process of job hunting tests your ability to do just that.

Compare yourself with Colin Jackson, the world champion hurdler. Each step in the job hunt is another hurdle to be overcome. Putting a CV together is one, responding to an announcement is another, completing the application on time is a third, and so on. So, write a note in your diary under 5 March: "papers to Tremendo, plc". Getting them in on time is a hurdle. It would be a pity to forfeit an opportunity out of carelessness, simply because you sent a CV without a letter of interest or because you didn't get the application back to the company on the day on which the advertisement indicated it should be in their offices.

To whom do you send your paperwork? An office, a box number, a contact person or job title will be listed at the bottom of most ads. Sometimes the company name is not included, because the ad may have been placed by an agency or corporate recruiter. If, however, the name of the company is listed without a specific name but with only the job title of the person to whom your application should be sent, such as the Personnel Director or Marketing Director or Sales Manager, make the extra effort and phone the office which placed the ad and ask for that individual's name. For example, if the ad says, "Personnel Director, Tremendo, plc", phone Tremendo and ask for the Personnel Director's name. Let's assume that you are told it's Mr Martin O'Brien. Address your paperwork to him. In this way, your letter will be delivered directly to him, and he may register the fact that you cared enough to invest some extra time to research the information — his name. With a minimum of effort, you will have differentiated yourself from some of the other applicants.

If you are using ads to find out about job openings, be sure to read more than one paper or magazine. Don't rely only on one source, for example, *The Irish Times* or *Sunday Business Post*. Different announcements may appear in different publications. Moreover, you will undoubtedly notice that at different times of the year ads for some industries decline or increase because the business is seasonal. For example, you will more than likely find fewer openings in the catering industry in Ireland in November than you will before the summer tourist season starts. And in the run-up to Christmas there may be a need for short-term or temporary help in retail, while other sectors do not advertise at that time because people wait for year-end bonuses before making career moves. In other words, become sensitive to the hiring patterns of the field or fields which interest you.

Checking Job Postings

If you are following periodicals for job announcements, then you should also be checking bulletin boards, flyers and newsletters located in or associated with career guidance and placement offices, or which are distributed by the societies and associations to which you may belong or of which you may know. Listen for radio shows that announce jobs; some TV programmes do, too, and you may discover computer networks offering new sources of information as well. Newsagents, shop windows and office bulletin boards frequently have postings, some of which are for internal transfers and promotions. Ads in journals, newspapers and magazines can be expensive, so some companies without large budgets for recruitment will use less expensive methods such as posting notices on bulletin boards or in looseleaf binders as a means of advertising positions. So check those sources on a regular basis to see what may have come in.

If there is an interesting position for which you believe you are qualified, once again photocopy the ad or bulletin and record the date. Unlike using periodicals, there is an ancillary benefit to checking or talking with your placement officer or association secretary. If you become a regular customer, he or she may very well keep you in mind when something suitable comes in. In fact, rather than run ads, some companies simply phone association or school/college programme offices to ask if they can recommend someone who might be interested or available for a possible assignment. If you have stayed in touch, that association, society, or office may refer your name. If that should happen, don't forget to say "thank you". Even if this lead doesn't work, maybe

the next one will, and people like to help those who
acknowledge other's efforts on their behalf. The reverse
is also true. People may resent being used or taken for
granted, so always remember to say "thank you", in
person, by phone, or by note.

Using Agencies, Head-hunters, Recruiters

Maybe you have had friends who secured their jobs
through agencies and recruiters. Perhaps that is a good
route for you to take. The key word is "perhaps". You
will have a better idea whether or not it is a viable
approach for you if you understand why companies turn
to outside agencies. There are many reasons, but two
important ones are time and money. Some companies
prefer to have an outside agency identify a limited number of candidates to interview for a particular position,
rather than to place an ad in the paper and then have to
handle 100–200 responses.

For example, suppose Company X is looking for an
internal auditor who has worked in the Middle East and
who has retail experience. As you can imagine, this is a
highly specialised position. Company X believes that the
recruiters will have more success locating such an individual and can do the screening for them more cost
effectively than they could by placing an ad in the paper.
In other words, Company X prefers to use its resources
differently. They don't want to allocate staff to the reading, responding, screening and interviewing of multiple
candidates. Instead, the recruiting firm will have to lo-
cate the qualified candidates, screen them and then present only three or four viable choices to the company.

Understand that because recruiters are typically
asked to work on specialised positions, it is unlikely that

if you are a recent graduate or a career changer you will have much success working with such agencies. Sometimes you will, but the average organisation has files of CVs from recent graduates; they don't need to pay fees to recruiters. However, once you have some additional experience in your field under your belt, and you want to make a move, then recruiters can be of enormous assistance if you stay in touch with them and ask them to keep alert on your behalf. From their vantage point they know what's happening in the market as well as the differing work environments and styles of management. Recruiters earn their reputations by the accuracy of their matches; that means identifying the right candidate for the right position in the right company in the right time-frame. Keep clear in your own mind what kind of environment is right for you, and let your personnel counsellor or career guidance officer know.

Sending Mass Mailings

Some job hunters grow weary of waiting for ads to appear in the papers and, unlike Simon, want to be more assertive. These applicants decide to be more proactive, and choose to put their names and backgrounds forward. They draft a generic letter introducing themselves, detailing their skills or recent accomplishments, which they photocopy and send with or without a CV to the top 1,000 companies or to every company which is a member of a particular professional association or to every company which appears under a particular heading in the *Golden Pages*. Getting your name out is certainly a more proactive approach than waiting for the papers; however, a general "Dear Sir or Madam" letter to 1,000 companies cannot, by definition, be targeted to meet an organisation's unique culture and needs.

Mass mailings are expensive in terms of postage and photocopying, and unless you can use a mail merge, it will be painstaking to address the letter to the actual name of the individual, rather than to Marketing Managers and Personnel Directors. The recipients in the organisation are going to recognise that this letter is part of a mass mailing, and although they may be impressed with your effort, they can, with reasonable accuracy, presume that you are not really interested in their particular organisation and its unique needs, but rather in getting work somewhere, anywhere in the field. There's nothing wrong with that approach, but organisations, like people, want to know that you care about their uniqueness, too. Though, of course, if you get a bite and an offer, the gamble will have paid off!

Networking

Networking is basically using who you know, and who they know, to uncover job possibilities. It is more proactive than newspaper scanning and more successful than mass mailings. Let's look at how it can work.

A recent graduate, Brian, may be convinced that he knows no one who can help him find a job. He has never met a bank president, a television producer or a government official. But suppose he wants to work in finance. First, he should use another page in his refill pad to make a list of all the people whom he knows: shopowners, classmates, friends, family members, parents of classmates, teachers, coaches, club advisors, members of the clergy, doctors. Once he has the list, he then needs to think about what their connections may be and whom they might know. For example, he may remember that his friend David Brown's dad is a banker, or that his classmate Stephen's mum is a professor of accountancy, or that someone with whom he plays football spent the summer working in a brokerage house in New York. Even though Brian believes that he doesn't know any people in his chosen field, he actually does. What he needs, though, is to have the courage and the confidence to approach one, two or three of them for advice. He is making connections; one leads to another which leads to another which leads to another. It is a matter of asking Stephen if he could talk to his mum, or asking David if his dad might be willing to give him some advice, or asking his football mate if he remembers any names at the brokerage house.

What Brian wants from each of these contacts is advice or direction or another name. He's not asking any of them for a job. If Brian asks David directly if he thinks his dad might have a job for him at the bank, the conversation may end right there. However, if Brian asks David if he thinks his father might give him some advice and then asks David for his dad's title because he wants to write a letter or make an appointment to ask for advice about careers in banking, the conversation probably will not end.

By and large, most people enjoy giving advice, helping and guiding. Let's suppose Brian meets Mr Brown — David's dad — or arranges to chat with him by phone. Mr Brown may advise Brian to read certain articles or contact a particular association that Brian did not know existed, or he may give him the name of someone in another financial institution who may be in the market for a recent graduate. The same may be true of Stephen's mum or of his old football friend. They are all leads. Leads. Leads. Leads.

Record the name, address and phone number of every potential contact and follow them all up. Each connection may lead to others, ergo: networking. Again, don't forget to thank every person who gives you a helping hand or a new direction. You may meet each one again. Sure, many of the leads will take you nowhere, and the process can be wearying, but you will be amazed when a journal's name is repeated, or you learn of a useful seminar, or you are given an individual's name which had been mentioned to you before in an earlier conversation. Wouldn't it be nice to phone that person and say "Mr Brown and Mr Green suggested that I speak to you"? In the process, you are not only learning more about the business but you are also making additional connections. Keep track of those leads and follow up on them.

Be sure to keep your original friends, your mentors or advisors informed. Don't be a pest, but even a casual remark helps: "Mr Brown, I want to thank you for introducing me to Mr O'Neill. He suggested that I talk with Mr Rose of X, and he is introducing me to Mr Jones who may have some openings." By being polite and professional you are also reminding Mr Brown that you are still looking for a position. In fact, he may have another idea. Networking takes energy, follow through, time and patience. But it does work.

Writing "On Spec"

Another approach may or may not be connected to networking. Suppose Mr Brown has given you a lead or you read the article in *The Economist* that he suggested. As a result, you decide to write a letter to the person or the company referred to in the article, without having seen a job announcement. That type of letter is targeted. Although, you don't know if there are any openings at the company, you are introducing yourself at Mr Brown's suggestion and describing your abilities as they relate to the article you read. And there is always a possibility that even if there is no opening today, there might be one later. Your CV might be attractive. You may intrigue them with your talents. They may be impressed with your proactive approach; they may even think of a possible opening.

As always, there is a continuum of responses to letters, from none at all to "thank you, no thank you", to "we will keep you on file", to "there may be an opening in several months", to — the one you want — "let's talk". If there's an interview, great, but if it's any of the others, open your diary to two months from now and write yourself a note to phone the person who signed the letter. Remind him or her of your previous letter expressing interest, and of the answer. Also keep a record of the name of the person who signed the letter you received. When you phone back, ask for him or her directly and request an exploratory interview.

If you have no specific contact name when you write a letter on spec, decide which office to write to. Should it be to personnel, the managing director or the manager of the department in which you want to work? Your decision should be based in part on the size of the organisation. For instance, not all companies have personnel departments. Furthermore, you may assume that personnel receives more post from people looking for jobs than the sales manager does. Consequently, you might have more success in writing to him or her because your letter would be different from the letters that the sales manager usually receives.

Attending Milk Rounds, Fairs, Expos, Conferences

Be aware of announcements of milk rounds, job fairs, expos or conferences. Each time you put your name forward, complete an application, or meet a corporate representative or recruiter, you learn something new. You can collect business cards, get names, read, ask questions. In essence, it's all part of your growing network.

At a fair or conference, as you walk past exhibition booths, you get a feel for who is hiring whom and what the companies are looking for in a candidate. You can also get a sense of the culture of the organisation by talking to some of the people there, a representative from an international consulting house, a recruiter from a manufacturing company, a marketer from a pharmaceutical house. The more you can learn, the better it is for you.

By participating in the milk rounds you can also improve your interviewing techniques, if you are called, which will make you better able to respond to future questions. You can collect, read and compare brochures and applications. At the same time, while you are learning about companies, you are also in a position to take a look around at your competition. You can talk with the others who are taking advantage of the meetings.

Walking in and/or Volunteering

Another job-hunting technique worth considering is to walk in to a company and volunteer. Suppose you have identified a specific company in an industry in which you want to work. Visit the company. Speak to someone at the front desk and ask for either the person involved in hiring or the person in charge of the department in which you want to work. The possibility is that such people are too busy to speak to you, so you may be asked to leave a CV. Get names and be assertive — but polite. Make an appointment. If you do meet anyone in authority, explain that you want to work in the company so badly that you are prepared to work for nothing for a week or longer to give the company the opportunity to see what you are capable of doing. Sound crazy? You'll have to sell yourself to be given the chance, and it is a big risk. You may be exploited as free labour, but many people have been hired for having the courage and in- genuity to take such a risk which gave them the oppor- tunity to display their talents. Also, by volunteering, you may end up being in the right place at the right time when an opportunity comes up. And, of course, at the very least you will gain valuable experience which could be useful later on.

Getting Temporary Assignments

Frequently companies or organisations have short-term projects lasting a few weeks or a month or two. There is often a need to cover for someone on leave, or the orga- nisation may be moving into job sharing. The resulting temporary job slots are golden opportunities for you to demonstrate your abilities as well as for you to see if you have found the right place. Don't forget: every work opportunity adds to your experience. And often temporary assignments can lead to full-time positions.

Putting it Together

So, clearly, you have a number of options. Ideally, couple your reading of the papers and checking

announcements with your networking and letter writing.
If you see an ad in the paper that looks appealing, a
member of your network may know someone at the
company who could tell you more about the position or
who could ask the company to consider interviewing
you. When you go to the milk rounds, or expos, take
names. Make phone calls, write letters introducing yourself, asking for interviews. Remember that not every job
is announced publicly, nor is every job planned for.

As was said earlier, sometimes knowing that a particular individual with certain talents to offer is available
leads an employer to undertake a project which up to
now has been on the long finger or to pull pieces of
positions away from already overloaded staff. But that
possibility will not happen if employers don't know that
you are out there looking for work. If you depend solely
on reading ads, employers can't know you are available.
On the other hand, others choose to announce their
availability for work by running their own ads, "position
wanted", or by buying space on billboards, or — as one
man did — by standing by the motorway holding a
placard announcing his background and availability.

The key is to be proactive and creative. Read the
papers. Study bulletins. Stay in close contact with
careers officers or societies to which you belong. Read,
watch, talk. Introduce yourself. Ask for advice. Find out
who is hiring whom. Walk in. Volunteer. Job hunting
involves a lot of hard work. It requires patience, determination and the courage to say that you're good. While
you are doing all that, you had better have taken time to
put your CV together, because everyone is going to be
asking for a copy. Let's now look at what makes an
effective CV.

Chapter 3

PUTTING YOUR CV TOGETHER

Your CV — Curriculum Vitæ or résumé — is an important document. It represents you. If there is no other initial human contact, the CV, your history, introduces you to a prospective employer by detailing and explaining your qualifications, your education, your work experience, your interests and achievements. Those pages are all that the company may know or remember about you, so, coupled with your covering letter, which will be discussed in Chapter 4, the CV must be designed to sell you and to do so quickly and well. Why "quickly"? It is important to realise that the average CV is initially reviewed in under 60 seconds. Why "well"? Like any other first impression, you need to make it a good one. Although it's read quickly, a good CV takes time to write. Be prepared to draft it a number of times until it looks good and includes essential information. Ultimately, it's yours to create.

General Guidelines

Before looking at a few models of CVs, let's examine some general guidelines which you should consider, a number of which may surprise you. Remember also that you should have more than one version of your CV; one if you are applying outside the country, and another for positions within it, and one or two others if you are

37

open to different kinds of positions, such as marketing or selling or teaching.

Keep it Short

CVs should be short and to the point. Although there are those who still like the four or five-page CV, in general the lengthy CV is on the wane. Unless you are an academic with 20 years of publications to put forward to an interview board, the business CV should be no more than one or two pages. There are those who would argue that the CV should be only one page. It's not possible, you say? Yes it is. First of all, rid yourself of the cover page which says "Curriculum Vitae" in the middle — that is one page easily eliminated. A CV looks like a CV, you don't need to announce the fact that it is one. Also disperse with the beautiful covers and bindings. Your stationery shop will make enough money on paper, photocopying and envelopes as it is. Covers are expensive, increase your postage and are a nuisance for a recruiter who wants to file or photocopy your material.

Use Phrases, Not Sentences

Needless to say, to fit your background into one or two pages, you are going to have to be clear and to the point. Therefore, use phrases not sentences. "I was living in Tokyo, and I spent my time translating reports into English" takes up more space than "translated Japanese reports into English".

Highlight your Selling Points

Does a prospective employer really need to know what all your marks were in your Leaving Certificate? It's enough to say you got your Leaving. For those of you in third level or who have completed it, why list all that second-level information when, by being accepted into third level, you have established that you have the necessary qualifications? You can always bring your marks with you to the interview, but on a CV they take up space, add clutter and don't reflect your talents. Sure, there is someone you know whose interviewer insisted that the marks be included. You can always have them on a separate page if you insist on having them, but not up front. Remember: quick first impression.

Make it Easy for the Interviewer to Find you

Speaking of space and selling points, your personal statistics don't require a full page either. What employers need to know is how to find you, if they want to, so your addresses and phone numbers or contact numbers should be right at the top of page 1.

Minimise Personal Data

It is not necessary to include on your CV your marital status, your sex, even your birth date or the state of your health. If, however, you feel strongly that one or any of those pieces of information is an important fact, then include it, but not on the top of your CV. Think about it! If this is a selling document which is scanned quickly, then what do you want to have jump off the page? What do you want the interviewer to notice first? Your B.Comm.? Your current job? Or your birth date?

Keep it Clear and Simple

Eliminate unnecessary words. For example, you sign your covering letter and application, not the CV. You've

eliminated the cover page which says "Curriculum
Vitae"; now eliminate those same words from the top of
the first page. Again, there is no need to label the obvious. A name looks like a name, an address like an
address. Therefore if your CV looks like the example
below, delete the words, "name" and "address":

> NAME: John O'Brien
> ADDRESS: 49 The Ravenswood
>   Dublin 4

Instead:

> John O'Brien
> 49 The Ravenswood
> Dublin 4

The additional words take up space and detract from the
important bits of information about you. Sure, you will
have to label some items, such as a home vs. term address, or office vs. home phone, but if you don't have to
add labels, don't. They increase clutter.

Design the CV so that it Appeals to the Eye

Your purpose is to make a first and, hopefully, a brilliant
impression. The document itself must be visually appealing; therefore, when it is finally ready to be laid out and
typed, you should select a type style that is easy to read.
In addition, you should select a good weight bond,
white or off-white paper. You should leave attractive
and balanced amounts of white space, so that the information is easy to read and the page looks user friendly.
Do you remember having to read horrible old text books
with two columns of small print on each page?

Avoid having three or four different kinds of type style — **bold**, *italics*, <u>**underlined bold**</u>, etc. The pages will look too busy and will defeat your purpose.

Check your Spelling and Typing

Although it may be startling to say this, it needs to be said: there should be no typographical or spelling errors in your CV. You would be amazed to know how frequent they are. One of the first reasons why a reader may put the CV in the "no thank you" pile is carelessness or inattention to detail. Please check that you did not attend "univeristy", or that you were not "invovled" in debating. You certainly do not have a "batchelor's" degree, nor do you "liase" with clients. One such spelling error and you are inviting rejection. In a recent real-life example, an applicant for an editing and proof-reading position had *five* typos in her CV. She did *not* get an interview.

An organisation wants to know not only that you can spell correctly but that your CV was put together with care. If you are sloppy or careless on your CV, you are signalling to the readers that you may be sloppy or careless in your work or in your person. Triple check for those kinds of errors. They'll cost you an interview, as they did for the proofreader.

Write from the Present to the Past

In terms of content, CVs should be written chronologically backwards. In other words, start from the present and work backwards, whether you are writing about your work experience, your educational background or your outside activities: the present to the past, not the past to the present.

Recruiters want to see easily and quickly what you are doing now. If they are interested, they will then read on to see where you have been. Keep remembering the impact of first impressions. After your name, what do you put next? Do you want the recruiter to remember that you were the Sugar Plum Fairy in your primary school play, that you are currently finishing a B.Comm. or a Master's, or that you have a driver's licence? — difficult as that is to get.

Be Specific

The content of the CV should be as specific as possible. If you supervised people in a previous job, indicate how many: two, three or 400? If you were responsible for a budget, was it £100, £50,000 or £500,000? If you sold, did you merely increase sales or did you increase sales by 25 per cent? By giving details you will paint a clearer picture of what you did, and provide more meaningful information for your prospective employers.

Avoid Gaps

Be sure that there are no unexplained gaps in your background. You don't want the reader to wonder where you were from 1983 to 1986. On safari? At home? In prison? On a yacht?

Tell the Truth

CVs should be honest. It may be tempting to increase the number of your years of experience or education by giving yourself credit for working somewhere that you have not worked, or by giving yourself a title or responsibilities that you really did not have, or by explaining a gap in employment by indicating that you worked for your uncle for a year when you did not. But don't succumb to those temptations. Sure, there are people who have done so and who get away with such tactics, but if you are one of the unlucky ones who is found out in the interview, in the reference check or even after you have been hired, you will regret it profoundly. You may find yourself dismissed for dishonesty and that is a stigma which will follow you. Believe that you'll be hired on your merit. Be patient.

Keep your CV Current

Any time there is a change in your life, be it work, education, name or address, bring your CV up to date. The day after you are awarded a certificate or get a promotion, alter your CV. If you move or if your phone number changes, update the CV.

Put your Name on Every Page

Suppose you have a two or three-page CV, and you plan to staple it in the upper left-hand corner. Be sure to type your name on the upper right of pages 2 and 3. For example: "O'Carroll, page 2". It's a small point, but if your CV is one of many or if it is being photocopied for circulation to other readers, pages can be confused. Aid the interviewer by writing your name on each page, unobtrusively.

Maintain a Balance

When you are drafting your CV, notice whether you have given five years of experience at one job more space than your summer position. Presumably what you

learned and accomplished in five years warrants more
space than what you did in two or three months. The
same is true of special interests or activities. Although
putting on *Riders to the Sea* in secondary school was a
highlight, does it require four lines, when your
B.Comm. is getting only one?

Sections of the CV

Those are some general guidelines. Now let's examine
what you might choose to write in all the sections of a
CV. Typically a chronological CV includes any or all of
the following: heading, objectives, education, experience, achievements, interests, other special information
and references/referees.

The Heading

The heading gives your name and address and where
you can be reached easily. You certainly don't want to
interest a company and then not give them an address or
a telephone number where you can be found. And since
telephone numbers can be confused with postal or zip
codes, label whenever it's necessary to avoid confusion.
For example, a heading might be:

Brendan Aherne
The Mews
Bray, Co. Wicklow
Telephone: 281 2345

If Brendan decides that he wants to send the CV out of
the country, he will need to provide additional information for the reader:

Brendan Aherne
The Mews
Bray, Co. Wicklow
Ireland
Telephone: 353-1-281 2345

Perhaps Brendan is working most of the day and doesn't mind receiving a phone call at work. He may write:

Brendan Aherne
The Mews
Bray, Co. Wicklow
Home Telephone: 281 2345
Office Telephone: 661 2345

If he does mind being phoned, he may write "after 6" next to his home number.

Brendan may be living on campus during term so he has two addresses:

Brendan Aherne

Home Address	Term Residence
The Mews	97 Student Hall
Bray	UCG
Co. Wicklow	Co. Galway
Tel: 281 2345	Tel: 091-12345

The Objectives

Like so much about CV writing, there are different schools of thought about stating objectives. There are those who believe that including one assists the reader in knowing more precisely what the candidate wants.

Others believe that an objective is unnecessary because the covering letter says it all. If you elect to include an objective you may want different CVs with different objectives for different types of positions and/or industries. Typically, the objectives are placed under the heading:

> Objective: An entry level position in marketing with an international manufacturing firm.

> or

> Objective: To have a responsible position in a financial institution enabling me to use my knowledge of economics.

> or

> Objective: To teach English to non-English-speaking students in Romania.

Education

If you do not yet have a significant amount of work experience, your education comes next on the page. As you acquire more experience, that order will probably be reversed. In other words, if you decide that your schooling is a bigger selling point for you than your work, then you put it first or vice versa. To repeat a point made earlier: each of your educational experiences should appear chronologically in reverse; each item should include the outcome, name of the institution, perhaps the location, and the dates. Decide, too, which is the most important part that should go first, that is, name of the college or university. The dates? The degree or certificate? More often than not, it is the degree that the company is buying, so:

MBA, Graduate School of Business, University College Dublin, Dublin, Ireland, 199x.

or

B.Comm., First Honours, University College Cork, Cork, 199x–9x.

or

Bachelor of Business Studies. University of Limerick. 199x–Present.

or

Dublin City University, Bachelor of Business Studies, 199x. Specialisation: Marketing.

or

Leaving Certificate, St Malachi's, Tipperary, 199x.

Again, if the CV is going out of the country, you cannot assume that Tipperary or Limerick are familiar to all your readers, so add the name of the country. Whatever pattern you choose, lay it out and punctuate it consistently. If you choose commas or full stops, each listing should match.

MBS. Graduate School of Business, University College Dublin, Dublin, Ireland, 199x.

B.Comm. with honours, University of Limerick, Ireland, 199x. Specialisation: Accountancy.

If the entry takes two lines, notice how the use of the tab or indent allows the first letters or word to stand out. If you are currently undertaking a course, then include it but where the date should appear write "present". Remember, as soon as the degree is awarded, update your CV.

Work Experience or Work or Professional Experience

Once again, this section is presented chronologically backwards with your most recent job first. And, as with your listing under education, there is a pattern for each position. It might be: job title, company, location, (if it matters), dates and responsibilities. What would make location matter? If you want the reader to see that you have had experience working in different countries, then it matters. If you worked in New York or Paris or Lugano, say so, but there is rarely a need to write the actual street address, like 23 Grafton Street, or 18 Kildare Street, or 101 Park Avenue.

To complete this section on work, think of all the jobs you have held. Having completed your self-audit, these should be readily available and fresh in your mind. Early in your career, you should include every position. Over time, some jobs may be dropped off the CV because after you have had a few years of experience under your belt, you will no longer need to include the fact that you worked weekends at a pub or worked as an au pair in Santa Fe, New Mexico. Such jobs become less relevant as your career develops.

However, do not automatically exclude those weekend and summer jobs you had in your early years. Those positions indicate to the employer that you are flexible, willing to put in long hours and understand what hard work means. In particular, do not exclude them if they directly relate to the positions you are after. For example, pub experience is a plus if you are applying for any jobs involving contact with clients or customers or in any area of catering or tourism.

When you describe your current position, do so in the present tense. When you no longer are doing the job or involved in the activity, then write it in the past. Currently, you "design" brochures, while in your last position you "designed" brochures. As was mentioned earlier, use specific references whenever possible. However if you consulted on a special market research project for Widget, Inc. just write "Manufacturing Co." instead of Widget, to avoid violating Widget's need for confidentiality. Prospective employers will recognise that in the future you're more likely to honour their need for confidentiality as well.

The self-reflection that you did before you started drafting your CV is invaluable now, particularly when you begin to describe the duties or responsibilities that you had. And try to think of them all. An entry in the "work" section might look like this:

Sales Assistant, Spector's, Waterford, 199x–Present.
  Responsibilities: Meet and greet customers,
  maintain inventory, handle customer complaints,
  write weekly reports, supervise one stock person.

Sales Assistant, White's Gift Shop, Dungarvan,
  Ireland, Summer 199x.
  Responsibilities: Served customers, wrapped
  packages, arranged for deliveries, phoned
  suppliers, kept daily accounts.

Clerk, Dungarvan Savings Bank, Dungarvan,
   Summers 199x–9x.
   Responsibilities: Maintained records, reported to
   the assistant manager, entered data into the
   computers, trained in foreign exchange.

During your career if you have held several full-time
jobs and several part-time ones, you may want two
headings:

Work Experience: Full-time
Sales Assistant, Spector's, Waterford, 199x–Present.
   Responsibilities: Meet and greet customers....

Work Experience: Part-time
Sales Assistant, White's Gift Shop, Dungarvan,
   Ireland, Summer 199x.
   Responsibilities: Served customers....

or

Work Experience

Full-time
   Sales Assistant, Spector's, Waterford, 199x–Present.
   Responsibilities: Meet and greet customers....

Part-time
   Sales Assistant, White's Gift Shop, Dungarvan,
   Ireland, Summer 199x.
   Responsibilities: Served customers....

Notice that when you write in this section, as we saw
earlier, you don't use full sentences. Start your phrases
with action verbs, and use the language of business to
describe the activities in which you were involved. Here

are some samples of verbs that you might want to consider. There are more, but these should give you the idea:

– organise	– supervise	– evaluate
– develop	– hire	– motivate
– plan	– create	– maintain
– design	– communicate	– recommend
– initiate	– implement	– train
– delegate	– administer	– research
– budget	– classify	– negotiate

As you draft your CV, you may notice that the same key word appears frequently in one section. For example, "organise meetings, organise conferences, organise travel plans". Combine these items for greater effect: "organise meetings, conferences and travel plans" or "organise meetings and conferences, and schedule travel".

Achievements

This section, like the statement of objectives, is an optional category. It can include awards, prizes, involvement in special events, etc. And you can find these on your refill pad under "social" or "leisure", such as,

- Chaired first All Ireland Conference on Debating
- Elected Class President at St Malachi's
- Organised Inter-School Singing Contest
- Named "Housewife of the Year"
- Member of Dramsoc
- Recipient of the Quinn Award for Tennis
- Co-Chair of the Community Welfare Committee
- Awarded 2nd Prize in the County Art Forum

Decide how to organise these items and then, to save space, if you "chaired" a number of events you may want to group the items: "Chaired the Conference on Debating, the Committee on Clean Air and the meeting on Housing for Senior Citizens" or if you are a member of a number of clubs or societies, rather than have a long list that fills half a page, run the items together Member of Debating Society, History Club, Bridge Club, Dramsoc.

Interests

If you choose to include a category entitled "interests", you are giving evidence that you are a well-rounded individual and may list activities such as reading, fishing, film, sports, handwork, travel, etc. Be consistent in your choice of parts of speech. Use all "ing" words or don't use them. For example, reading, fishing, watching films, playing rugby, etc., rather than as they are listed above.

Important warning: During the interview be ready to discuss the interests that you have written on the CV. If you wrote that you travel or read, or go to films, a good interviewer will undoubtedly ask you where you travelled or what you've read or what you thought of the last film you saw.

Additional Information

You may have knowledge of certain computer languages or foreign languages or specific accounting procedures that you have not recorded elsewhere in the CV. Such specialist training skills should be cited in this section. Therefore:

Special Training

Knowledge of French, Spanish
Speaking knowledge of Dutch
SPSS, Cobol, Basic, Fortran

Referees

Before discussing what to write in this section of your CV, let's underline the importance of your referees and why and how you should choose them and then why you should protect them. Simply stated, your referees put in a good word for you; they vouch for you. Referees may be anyone: doctors, businesspeople, lawyers, teachers, clergy, friends, etc. You may have known them for years or as a result of some recent networking. Whoever you select — and you may use different referees for different types of positions in different industries — never assume that you may use someone as a referee without their permission. Ask first! If you get permission, ask them what name and address and telephone number you may give to the interviewer. Then, when you are a finalist or serious candidate, advise your referees that you are one of the last two or three and that Mr or Ms So and So from the company may be contacting them.

In addition to getting permission to use their names, it is important to protect your referees from excessive contact. Don't forget, if you are applying for many jobs, your referees may be contacted frequently. In addition you are probably not the only person using their names. For example, suppose you have selected someone in the public eye or an administrator from your school;

multiply your phone calls by the number of phone calls from others who may also be using them as referees. Consider their time and privacy. Use referees prudently, but, at the same time, keep them informed of your progress and thank them afterwards for extending themselves for you. Referees don't enjoy being the last to know on hearing from a third party that you landed a job. You may want to use their names again for something else in a few years' time, so treat them politely.

What should you include on your CV about your referees? You can either write nothing, write "References/ Referees on Request", or write their actual names and contact phone numbers. Again, you may need multiple CVs with different referees: Mr Brown for banking positions, Prof. O'Neill for a lecturing position, and so on.

The format may look like this:

<u>Referees</u>:

Dr J. Jones
Professor of Electrical Engineering
Gloucester University
Gloucester UK GLI 2TN
Telephone: 0452-412-345

Mrs S. Byrne
CEO
The Megashop
Bridge Street, Galway
Telephone: 091-61234

Just as the lengthy CV is disappearing, so is the written reference. Nowadays there is greater use of the phone. Because the world is more litigious, however, and since people are more concerned with what may be considered libellous, fewer personal judgments are written. Even phone-callers are cautious. Respondents are becoming more prudent when asked about current or past employees, relying on an innocuous "Yes, he worked with us from _____ to _____", rather than on a subjective judgment about a former employee's work style.

Sample CVs

Now let us put it all together and look at some sample CVs. The following may give you some ideas of how to lay out your own:

SUZANNE CHAMBERS

110 New Road
Ballyconnell
Co. Cavan
Telephone: (049) 21234

EDUCATION

Bachelor of Commerce (Hons), University College Galway, 199x.

Leaving Certificate, St Bridget's Secondary School, 199x.

WORK EXPERIENCE

Research Assistant, The Serious Research Company, Dublin, Summers 199x-9x.

Duties: Conducted three personal interview studies, four telephone surveys. Assisted Senior Researcher with interpretation of the data for a feasibility study. Wrote draft reports. Attended client and staff meetings.

Sales Assistant, The Cute Boutique, Hyannis, MA USA, Summer 199x.

Duties: Worked with a team of three in a gift shop catering to tourists. Served customers. Maintained inventory. Totalled receipts daily. Stocked shelves.

ACHIEVEMENTS

At University College Galway:
Captained the Senior Tennis team. Won Connacht title in 199x.
Selected for the All Ireland Debate contest.
Member of the Research Society.

INTERESTS

Reading, Swimming, Tennis, Travelling.

S. CHAMBERS (P. 2)

REFEREES

Mr Michael Latour   Mr Fred Wilson
Owner   President
The Cute Boutique   The Serious
Ocean Drive   Research Company
Hyannis   44 Canal Road
MA 04321 USA   Dublin 9
Phone: 001-617-5012345   Phone: 661 2345

Professor Declan Reilly
Department of Marketing
UCG
Co. Galway
Phone: 091-61234

Stephen O'Loughlin

"Rose Villa"   Office: 971 2345
Rathmines, Dublin 6   Home: 765 4321

Professional Experience

Prudent Insurance Company

Senior Analyst   198x–Present

Co-ordinate activities of a three-person team; produce and
verify monthly and bi-monthly reports; design and implement
information systems for six regional offices, monitor
performance of sales offices; report to management; member
of a new product design committee; promoted from Trainee
position.

Trainee Analyst   198x–8x

Assisted management with reports; attended staff and client
meetings; collected and interpreted data.

Educational Experience

B.Sc.(Mgt), Trinity College, Dublin, 198x.

Additional Training

Certificate in Commercial French, Centre Commerciale, Paris,
France, 198x.
Harvard Graphics, Excel.

Interests

Photography, play football, tennis and squash.

Referees on Request

SEÁN McWILLIAMS

| 42 Castlepoint Road | Tel: (h) (098) 20123 |
| Castlebar, Co. Mayo | Tel: (0) (098) 21234 |

EDUCATIONAL BACKGROUND

MBS, Graduate School of Business, University College Dublin, 199x. Specialisation: Management Studies.
BComm, University College Cork, 199x.

PROFESSIONAL EXPERIENCE

Supervisor of Operations, Effective Manufacturing plc, Westport, Co. Mayo, 199x–Present.
Duties: Supervise 14 clerical and factory staff. Maintain records. Recruit, hire and evaluate employees. Establish work schedules. Set and monitor production goals. Maintain plant safety. Liaise with clients. Write reports. Serve on Management Team.

Assistant Personnel Officer, The Quality Business Co., Denver, Colorado, 199x–9x.
Duties: Responsible for the maintenance of personnel records. Entered information into data bank. Screened first-round candidates. Drafted advertisements. Assisted manager in the calculation of sick and personal time utilisation reports. Drafted job descriptions and classified advertising.

ACHIEVEMENTS

Named New Employee of the Year at The Quality Business Co.
Member: Business Society of Dublin, the Business Person's Network and the International Manufacturing Association.
Winner of the UCC Speaking Contest.

REFERENCES ON REQUEST

Notice the choices people have made. Suzanne has decided to put her education first and to include the name of her referees. Stephen O'Loughlin, you will notice, has a lot of work experience, so he has placed that first. Notice also that since he's had two positions with one organisation, the company is the heading with the two jobs as subheads.

There are other types of CVs, such as the functional CV, which create categories of talents, as in the following one which emphasises Management Skills, Communication Skills, and Training Skills rather than a listing of work experience. Such a format might be useful for someone who has been out of the job market for some time and whose work experience is limited.

Sheena Reed
6 Kenilford Drive
Larne, Co. Antrim
BT 40 2LB
Telephone: (0574) 212345

MANAGEMENT:

Led a team of 20 students who organised Open Day.
Administered the budget for a production of *Juno and
the Paycock.*
Planned a promotional campaign for the Dramsoc.

COMMUNICATION:

Spoke with local business people.
Wrote press releases, reports and articles for the school
paper.
Acted in secondary school and University productions.
Recruited new students for Dramsoc.

TRAINING:

Assisted secondary students in preparing for exams.
Taught English to three visiting French students.
Instructed new Dramsoc members in the use of lighting
board.

EDUCATION:

Queens University, Bachelor of Arts, 199x to Present.
Specialisation: World Theatre.
The Kenilworth School, Leaving Certificate, 199x.

WORK EXPERIENCE:

Summers 199x–9x, Waitress in Lough Inn, Larne, Co.
Antrim.

These are only sample CVs. Depending on your own unique experiences and education, decide which will best highlight the qualities that you want to sell to the company and what is the best way visually to lay them out. Developing a good CV is an essential element in the job-hunting process, and it takes time.

Your covering letter focuses the reader's attention on those parts of the CV you want to highlight, so now let's examine covering letters.

Chapter 4

WRITING A COVERING LETTER

The House
Rathphilip
Co. Dublin

5 March 199x

Mr Martin O'Brien
Personal Director
Tremendo, plc
The Cork Road
Douglas, Co. Cork.

Dear Sir,

I enclose my CV for your review. I look forward to hearing from you because I really want to work for you.

Yours sincerely,

John O'Carroll

Sorry, John. Not a chance! This letter is not going to open any doors. In fact, it may close one. Before we examine John's letter to see why, let's establish what a covering letter is meant to do and how it is usually organised. First of all, like your CV, this is a selling document, so it should be short and written to attract the reader's attention. It should include specific examples of what you have to offer the particular organisation, or state clearly what you have to offer, matching the requirements that have been detailed in an ad. If you are writing on spec, the contents of your letter should include what has prompted you to write, as well as what you have to offer.

Therefore, as in any other business letter, the opening paragraph explains your reason(s) for writing, the middle paragraph(s) should expand on those initial reasons by using examples to show how your experience matches the job requirements, and the closing paragraph should recommend a method for following up on this letter.

That three-part formula essentially organises the content of the standard covering letter. Like the CV, the layout, format, neatness and thoughtfulness must all reflect your professionalism. Individual covering letters should be written for every position for which you apply. Should it be typed or handwritten? Again, there are differing schools of thought and the decision is up to you. If you think that a handwritten letter is more personal, then do what you think is best. However, if your handwriting is atrocious, then there is no question. Type! Either way, it should be on quality paper and neatly presented.

Before looking at an example of an effective covering letter, let's examine John's to see some of the reasons why he may expect to find his letter in the "no thank you" file or the "we'll call you, don't call us" category.

The House
Rathphilip
Co. Dublin

5 March 199x

Mr Martin O'Brien
Perso<u>na</u>l Director
Tremendo, plc
The Cork Road
Douglas, Co. Cork.

Dear <u>Sir</u>,

<u>I</u> enclose my CV for your review. <u>I</u> look forward to hearing from you because <u>I</u> <u>really want to work for you</u>.

Yours since<u>rl</u>y,

John O'Carroll

John has two spelling errors: "Personal" and "sincerly". He has written "Dear Sir" even though he knows the name of the Director, Mr Martin O'Brien. He has overused "I" — three times in two sentences. Furthermore, in terms of the content, he has not sold himself, nor has he indicated what he has to offer the company. Clearly John forgot to think of AIDA. He failed to win Mr O'Brien's attention or interest. He also fails to specify what job he is applying for, probably confusing Mr O'Brien, who may have advertised six different jobs that week. And look at that final line! Is wanting to work for someone reason enough to be interviewed?

John can do better. Had he thought about it, he could

have come up with a variety of openings, just as you can. It takes time! Some of these samples are more conservative than others, but they can give you an idea. Here are some possible starters:

> "I am writing to apply for the position of Sales Trainee advertised in *The Irish Times* of 17 February."

> "Please consider this my application for the Assistant Brand Manager position which is posted in the career's office at the University of Leeds."

> "Last week an article in the *Cork Examiner* indicated that you were expanding your Belfast plant. I believe that my five years' experience with Longg's and my training in microcomputers would make me a valuable addition to your staff."

> "Damian Harvey, Manager of The Beta Sales Association, suggested that I write to introduce myself to you, because I am an excellent_____."

> "I can save you money, with my knowledge of cost accounting and_____."

> "The two summers that I spent as a teller in Cork Savings Bank will benefit your organisation, because_____."

Notice that in every case there is an explanation of why you wrote the letter and a brief indication that you have something to offer that would benefit the company. In each case you are specific about where you saw the ad or what prompted you to write. The next sentence might list your assets. Again the degree of flamboyance or conservatism projected in your letters has to do with your comfort level and your personality. Be yourself. Just remember to put your talents forward.

For example, if you are answering an ad, then you use the requirements that were listed in the paper or bulletin and let the reader know that you possess them. You then continue in subsequent paragraphs by giving concrete examples to prove that you do possess those abilities. Let's suppose you see an ad for an organisation that is seeking a person with "problem solving skills", an "ability to provide leadership" and "high energy". First, indicate that you have those abilities, if you do, and then provide specific examples demonstrating any or all of those talents. You might write:

"Please consider this my application for the position of Management Trainee advertised in the *Independent* on Friday, 4 April. I am qualified because I am a high energy individual who thrives on problem solving and who has also had experience in leadership roles. For example_____."

You then provide examples. Here are some:

Problem solving:

"When I travelled to France last summer, I arrived without a job and yet within a week I found work."

or

"A young man I supervised was having personal problems, and his work was deteriorating. However, I_____."

or

"I was able to attend university at night and still increase my sales by 10 per cent."

Ability to provide leadership:

"As captain of my rugby team (or hockey team), I_____."

"As head of an environmental committee, I was_____."

"There had been no money in our budget until I_____."

High energy:

"I can handle multiple projects at once. For example, while going to school, I worked weekends at_____ and still had time for sports."

"As a member of the Dramsoc, I was involved in putting on four money-making plays a year. Each one required casting, rehearsal, production, all on our own time."

"Although I worked full-time for the X Company, I completed my degree in Marketing."

In other words, provide specifics to support your claim that you meet each of the requirements Then, once you have indicated what you can bring to the job, move to a conclusion. This should make clear what you can do for the organisation and what action you want to take:

"As you can see, based on my training and experience, I would be an asset to the HRM department. Therefore, I would welcome the opportunity of talking with you. I will phone in two weeks to arrange a mutually convenient appointment."

or

"My marketing degree and the two summers I spent working in research should enable me to assist in the feasibility study. I would welcome talking more with you about the project."

or

"Given my knowledge of computers and my supervisory work with nursing home staff, I know I can solve your scheduling problem. I await your reply."

or

"As a result of my energy and effective communication skills, the new product would be launched successfully and on time. I'll call to your office next Friday morning to arrange a meeting."

In essence, the covering letter consists of three parts:

1. Why you are writing;
2. What you have to offer the company and why;
3. A conclusion that indicates what you want to have happen next.

A revised sample letter from John might look like this:

The House
Rathphilip
Co. Dublin

5 March 199x

Mr Martin O'Brien
Personnel Director
Tremendo, plc
The Cork Road
Douglas, Co. Cork.

Dear Mr O'Brien,

I am writing at the suggestion of Sean Dunne of the Sales Group, who indicated that you might have an opening for a sales trainee, a position for which I am ideally suited. Having worked as a sales assistant at Clery's for two summers and as a waiter at Mac Qs, in Martha's Vineyard in the United States, I have dealt directly with people and worked under pressure.

In both of those positions, I interacted with hundreds of people on any given day. Mac Q's is a popular fast food organisation. Clery's, on the other hand, caters to visitors to Ireland who enjoy more leisurely browsing. In both cases, I listened to customers and learned how to ask people what they were looking for and encouraged them to consider certain items. Rarely did a customer leave Clery's without spending at least £10 in my department. At both Clery's and Mac Q's the customers expected quality service. In fact, I earned the service award at Mac Q's.

With Tremendo's training, and these two work experiences, coupled with my interest in psychology and keen interest in competitive sport, I can develop into a high-earning salesperson.

I look forward to talking to you about the possibilities of my joining your firm and will phone next week to arrange an appointment.

Yours sincerely,

John O'Carroll

This revised sample covering letter highlights the selling points that John wants to emphasise for a sales trainee position. The letter also focuses the reader's attention on specific parts of the CV. He tells Mr O'Brien to note two particular summer jobs and his achievement — Mac Q's, Clery's and the service award. In your case, you might emphasise a project you completed, an after-school experience you have had, or an event you organised.

Once you have drafted and edited your covering letter so that it achieves what you want it to do, make a photocopy of it and write yourself a note in your diary indicating the date on which it was posted and the day you're going to phone, if you wrote that you would. John said that he would phone in two weeks. In two weeks John will phone Mr O'Brien at Tremendo, plc, to see what the status of his letter is.

A few words need to be said about phoning. All your conversations should be gracious and businesslike:

"Good morning. Tremendo Company. May I help you?"

"Good morning. This is John O'Carroll. Mr O'Brien is expecting my phone call."

"He's not available. He's in a meeting."
"When is a good time for me to reach him?"
"Tomorrow morning."
"Any time?"
"Before 10 o'clock is usually best."
"Would you please tell him that I phoned, and I'll try
    to reach him tomorrow before 10."
"I certainly will."
"Excuse me, but what's your name?"
"Eileen."
"Thank you, Eileen."

Alongside Martin O'Brien's name in his diary, John should write "receptionist or secretary, Eileen".

One caveat about covering letters. When you reread your draft letter, having corrected spelling and typographical errors, notice the frequency with which the pronoun "I" appears. If you find that the letter reads "I have worked _____ since I first _____ I have a _____ and I have good _____ I also have...", in other words, "I", "I", "I", "me", "me", "me", do some editing. See if you can combine sentences or structure them differently, such as:

"Since first managing the department, I have increased productivity and improved staff attendance."

rather than

"Since I first managed the department, I have increased productivity and I have improved staff attendance."

When you are happy with both your CV and your covering letters, show them to several people and ask for some feedback on the content and on the layout. Then, although pale pink and blue may be tempting because they are different, select white or off-white paper. There is no need to spend exorbitant sums on printing. Clear black print photocopied on good paper is sufficient. Instead, spend your money on quality paper, good bond, on postage and phone calls, on bus fares or petrol for going to libraries, interviews or seminars and conferences.

Like so much of job hunting, constructing a good CV and a good covering letter is hard work, but with them in hand you have increased the odds of getting in the door.

Chapter 5

COMPLETING APPLICATIONS

Whether you write to the company on spec or apply for a particular advertised position, many organisations respond to a covering letter and CV by sending you an application form to complete. Milk rounds or recruiting fairs are also a source of applications. If you view the hiring process as a series of hurdles that you have to jump in order to have a chance of winning, then completing application forms is just another one. Keep your goal in mind. What you are after is an interview.

Probably the biggest problem with completing applications is the emotional one. You receive a letter from the company you have written to, tear open the envelope and say "Ah no, why? I just sent them my CV! It's the same stuff, so why do I have to write it again?!" Your frustration with the necessity of completing an application saves the company time. A number of would-be candidates for a position quit right at this point. They screen themselves out. Completing the form is a bother they feel is too much work! Remember your objective? Work is what you are trying to get!

So, if the sight of an application form infuriates you, make the decision to fill it out or not to fill it out. And if you do make the former decision, do it right, not half-heartedly.

There are many symptoms of a poorly completed application. It is incomplete. Questions are left unanswered. Boxes are left blank. The form may be filled out in two different coloured inks. There are erasures or words crossed out or blobs of tipp-ex. There may be changes in handwriting. Sometimes the boxes are filled out in script and sometimes printed in block letters. Frequently, the line that calls for a signature is left blank or undated and many of the lines following questions such as "list your educational experience", say "see CV".

If you resent filling out the form or if you feel cavalier about it, then don't bother. You are wasting your own time and the company's, because if you don't make the effort to complete the form carefully, you may find that your application and your CV will be in that "no thank you" pile once again. So take your time and fill it in carefully. What you want is one more document, in addition to your covering letter and CV, which is neat, thoughtful and professional looking, just like you. Therefore, before you even put your name on the application, make a photocopy of the original and put it safely away in a drawer or in a folder for a while, so that it won't be creased, crumpled or coffee stained while you work on it. Read each question systematically, filling in each blank on your photocopy as you are instructed: "please print" or "hand write" or "type" or "print in bold letters". For longer answers, draft and edit them on pages of your refill pad before you transfer them to the original form.

Along with your CV, the completed application form will often become the basis for discussion during the interview, so answer the questions accurately and thoroughly. Start with the easy ones: your name, address, contact or telephone number. If you don't have a phone, indicate the number of someone who knows your whereabouts. Continue to fill in the blanks: the title of the job for which you are applying, your education, your experience, etc. Where the form calls for dates, the ones you write should coincide with those on your CV. Leave no lines or boxes empty.

Redesigning forms is not always a high priority for companies, so you may receive antiquated application forms which have not been updated for years. Therefore, you may find some inappropriate questions on the form asking for your age, sex, marital status, or previous salary — questions which it is no longer considered appropriate to ask. However, if you are confronted by questions that you consider intrusive and if you genuinely have strong feelings about responding to some of them, then you will have to take the decision to answer them or not. Depending on the perspective of the reader, if you choose not to answer, you may be knocked out of the running, but that is the chance you take. Then you may have to ask yourself whether you would fit in with that company anyway. However, if you do decide not to answer a particular question about your age or sex, be sure to put a line in the box indicating that you have read it. If you don't make some kind of mark or indication, the reader may think that you inadvertently or carelessly left it blank.

A problematic box or line on the form is one which may ask you to indicate what salary or wages you require. You can understand why there are problems involved in answering that question. If you write £8,000 as your required salary, for example, and the company is prepared to pay £14,000, you will have undersold yourself. On the other hand, if you write £35,000, and the company has planned to offer £20,000 plus benefits, you will have priced yourself too high. In the latter case, what can hurt is that you might be genuinely prepared to work for less because it is important for you to work in that particular industry, in that precise location or department, in that unique company or in that specialised training programme, or any or all of the above because of the long-term career implications. How do you answer what salary you want? There are a number of choices: "open" is one, "negotiable" is another or writing a realistic range, such as £6,000–£10,000, £15,000–£18,000 or £40,000–£50,000, is another. It's a difficult decision to make. You may want to speak to someone in your network who might advise you on what a fair salary might be for such a position in a particular industry. In some cases you have to take a longer term view than your starting pay.

If you haven't thought about it yet, now is a good time to think about what money you will or can afford to work for. At this stage of the job hunt, there is a natural tendency to focus on getting in the door of a company for an interview, rather than on the fact that with few exceptions — lottery winners, perhaps — we are all working to earn a living. So, it's important to calculate realistically what you need or can manage to live on, in both the short and longer term. Think about your responsibilities and obligations. Calculate your expenses: housing, transportation, food, clothes, baby minder, etc. Is it going to cost you to work? If you are worried about your debts, will you be able to focus on your job? Notice the word "realistically". Tickets to all World Cup matches, an apartment in Marbella or the latest Merc may not be on the cards yet. However, that doesn't mean that they won't be at a later date. Questions about salary and benefits are going to arise soon, so begin to do some thinking and calculating.

By now you have completed the easier bits on the application, the little boxes, but then it gets harder. There are questions that require more than one-word answers, so draft your responses on the refill pad. Like your CV and covering letter, let your drafts sit for a while. Come back to them later to see not only if the answer is adequate and grammatically correct, but also in a tone consistent with that of the question.

You may come across questions like:

"Why are you applying?"
"What accomplishment are you proudest of?"
"What are you least proud of?"
"What is your best attribute?"
"What was the biggest problem you had to solve? How did you solve it?"
"What is/was your favourite subject in school?"

Those are tougher than your name and phone number And you need to give yourself time to think about the answers and to do so in business terms. For example, let's take the question "What accomplishments are you proudest of?" Although you may be proudest of mitching from school for a week and not being caught, that is probably not an ideal response for an application question.

Take another look at your copy of the advertisement or the announcement. Think about what you know about the company, or about the type of position that you are seeking. Look back at your self-analysis notes and then dredge your memory to see if there is something you did that is appropriate for the company. Suppose the position involves research. Was there a difficult project that you completed, or a technical problem that you solved? If it's a people job, was there a team-mate whom you helped? If the working environment is pressurised, was there some complicated situation which you managed to juggle? Think of answers that suit business and the company.

At work, you will have to complete difficult projects, solve technical problems, assist a team member or juggle tasks. Companies are not looking for you to have won the Nobel Prize, a Grammy or every award in school. When they study your application, they are looking for your ability to articulate a reasonable, sensible appropriate business response. And bear in mind that now is the time to be political, not confessional. Yes, be honest, but also be smart. When the form calls for you to explain why you are applying for this position, don't write "because I need work", or "advertising seems like fun", or "I need a summer job". Those answers all may be true, just as your being proud of mitching may be true, but your good business sense is being examined as well. Is this company going to hire someone who "shoots from the hip" or lip? Maybe, but get in the door first. If you do answer that way, you will be asking to be put in the reject file again.

Learn from Suzanne's answer about wanting to travel: put the company's needs first. What do they want? Think of John's revised covering letter. He's applying because he enjoys selling and believes that with additional training he'll be better at it and will make the company money. Perhaps you are applying because you have "been fascinated by aeroplanes" all your life, or perhaps you are applying because you "have the technical skills" to do the job. Sell the talents that you have which will be a plus to the organisation, but keep the hirer — the buyer — in mind as you answer.

It was said earlier, but it needs to be said again: tell the truth. If you did not work for IBM, don't write on the application that you did. We all know that it is a burden to lie. You have to remember what you said, and you may find yourself worrying that someone will find out. All of that energy detracts from your performance. Get the interview on your merits, on the truth, not on an expedient fiction. And that caveat relates to accuracy of dates and titles, too. If you worked two months at a job, don't write two years. If you were a barmaid, please don't write that you managed the place.

Near the end of the application you will probably be asked for names of your referees. As with your CV, select them wisely. Pick people who you know have some relationship to the position for which you are applying or to the industry. For example, your lecturer in accountancy might be a better choice than your lecturer in literature for an accounting firm, while the reverse might be true for a publishing company. In other words, make a prudent selection.

All of your answers will have been written in rough copy. Let them sit for a while. Then polish your language: combine sentences, check your grammar, punctuate and spell correctly. Now transfer your answers to the original form carefully. And follow instructions: print, hand write, type; do what the form tells you to do. Remember, erasures do not belong on an application. If you find that what you have written does not fit on the lines or in the box provided, then do what most applications suggest that you do, "use another sheet of paper", another good piece of bond. Just be sure that you put your full name on any and all others, and that you number your answer(s) to coincide with the question(s) for which you required more space. Here's a small point. If you elect to hand write extra application pages, place a piece of lined paper underneath the plain bond. Your work will be neater. Rather than have your handwriting slope up or down or have unequal spacing between lines, you'll have a tidier piece of work to submit. Now reread the application. Check the "p"s and "q"s, the full stops, the apostrophes where needed. Check that every question is answered, or that a line is drawn through those you do not want to answer, if there are any. Then, if the form calls for a signature, PLEASE SIGN IT! It is heart breaking to see an application which is carefully and thoughtfully completed but lacks a required signature and date. Remember: attention to detail is part of what the job search is about.

Once you have completed the application to your satisfaction, photocopy it. Write a note in your diary indicating when you posted it to the company or dropped it off at the front desk. Now forget about it, and look for another door to open. If three or four weeks pass and you have not heard, phone the company's contact person — you have the name — indicating when you posted the application and then ask the status of the screening process. Jot down in your diary that you phoned on a certain date and with whom you spoke. In the meantime, while you are waiting for a response, keep your eyes open, keep reading and talking and expanding your network. Send off another CV with another covering letter and start thinking about getting ready to be interviewed. Although you may not believe it, with more good covering letters, CVs and applications out, you will eventually be called for an interview.

Chapter 6

PREPARING FOR INTERVIEWS

Play out this scenario: Of seven covering letters and CVs that you have sent out so far, you have received five "no thank you" letters and two invitations to be interviewed. Bravo! Keep these "no thank you"s for future reference. Why? Suppose one letter indicated that the company is not hiring now, remember that they might be in the future. So, down the road you may want to write a letter to the person who signed the "no thanks" letter, indicating that you had written earlier and what the response was. However, there is work to be done now. You have two interviews. Tremendo, plc, has written to you asking that you be in their offices in Douglas at 10 a.m. on Thursday week and to confirm the appointment. In addition, Microtech phoned you to arrange a mutually convenient time. So what do you do now?

Questions to Ask

When you phone to confirm the appointment with one company and arrange a time to meet with the other, you should take the opportunity to ask a few questions. Interviewing is stressful because the possibility of being offered a position is important to you, so the less you have to worry about the better. Having a few details in advance of the meeting eases some of the pressure. So, here are some things you may want to know:

1. How long will the interview last?
2. Exactly where should you report?
3. With whom will you be interviewing?

How long will the interview last?

It is helpful for you to know if the organisation intends to keep you for 30 minutes, for half a day, or for a whole day. Thus, you will know whether to keep your whole day clear or to reschedule some other appointments. You certainly don't want to be in an interview that you assumed was for an hour and learn that the interviewer wants you to stay for half a day. You could find yourself under additional pressure if you have to go to a dentist's appointment or have arranged to meet someone for lunch. Sometimes interviewers will ask if you would like to walk around the offices or plant, or if you have a few minutes to meet with Mr So and So. You don't want to be torn between your other obligations and a possible job. In addition, some organisations may schedule assessment tests for which you will want to be available, so ask in advance how long you should plan to spend with them. You will be more at ease on the day.

Where do you report?

In your excitement at being invited to an interview, don't forget to ask exactly where you should go. Sure, you know the address: Tremendo, plc, on the Cork Road in Douglas. But precisely how do you get there, and exactly where in the building should you go? It

sounds silly, but sometimes what looks straightforward
is not. Industrial estates can be mazes. Bus stops and
train stations can be several miles away. If you are
staying overnight with relatives, will they be able to
drop you off or will you need to phone for a taxi? Is
there public transportation? How often does the bus or
train run? Even if the company is in your own town, the
location may be unfamiliar to you. There may be one-
way streets or disc parking only. You certainly don't
want to be late or perspiring because you didn't have
the precise directions, because you didn't realise that the
main door was down the lane. Some offices have side
entrances or annexes, so besides a precise set of
directions, you should also ask what door you enter,
what floor to go to or whom you should ask for. Jot it
down in your diary.

Who is doing the interviewing?

It is also useful to know who is doing the interviewing,
their name(s) and job title(s). Although there may have
been some phone calls, up to now most of your effort
will have involved exchanging paper. Now you're talking to people. And like any presentation, the more you
know about them, the better. Will it be someone from
the personnel department? Will it be the manager of the
department in which you would work? Would it be your
immediate supervisor or is it a panel of people and, if
so, who are they? What are their names? What's their
relationship to the organisation and to the particular
position? You might try to find out a little about the
person or persons. Are they new to the company? Have
they been there for years? You can then go back into
your network and see who knows what about whom.

With those questions answered, let's assume you have arranged the details, noted them in your diary, planned the route and, if the company is local, actually done a practice run so you know how much time you need to get there with a few minutes to spare. Now you need to anticipate some of the questions that you might be asked during the interview.

Preparing for the Interview

First of all, do some research on the company. If there are annual reports, brochures, or flyers available, request them or go to the library and look for them. If the company has recently been in the newspaper, look up past articles. Is there a potential acquisition? Have they successfully launched a new product? See what you can find out. If you uncover something newsworthy, then be ready to have an opinion about it. For example, if they've recently launched a new biscuit, have you seen it? Have you tasted it? Do you like it? You might be asked. Do some homework on the industry in general. Is it going through a change? Is the competition changing? What are the implications for the company of technology or new government regulations or position papers?

In addition to reading about the company and researching the industry, in the days prior to the interview, talk to people. Use that network of yours. What do people know about the industry or the company or the management? Do you know someone who works there or for a competitor or a supplier or a client? Make a phone call, have a coffee and chat. Or if you know someone who has a similar job title in another company of comparable size, find out about their responsibilities, the support systems, the organisational structure, the problems. Can you learn something about your inter-viewers? Can you uncover that one of them is an extremely nice man, or that Mr Johnson can be "sarky" to MBAs or that Ms Riley dislikes women who are re-turning to the job market? Do you know anyone who was recently hired by them and might be willing to share some interview experience with you?

As well as getting background information, take out your CV, your covering letter and your application and read what you wrote. What did you emphasise in your covering letter? John needs to bring his experiences at Clery's and Mac Q's clearly back to his mind. You need to remember what you did, how you spent your day, what your colleagues were like, your boss. Bring the images and experiences back, so you will be able to respond to the questions with real-life examples to support them.

You also should decide what to wear. What clothes make you look neat and professional? Do you have to have new heels put on your shoes? Does your suit need a cleaning or pressing? In interviews you are usually seated next to or across from your interviewer. You are close, so be sure that your blouse or shirt is ironed, that your hair is neat, that your fingernails are free of the dirt from playing ball, fixing a bike or potting a plant. Avoid onion sandwiches, heavy colognes, aftershaves or perfumes.

Some applicants wonder what they should wear if they are applying to a creative industry such as advertis-ing or PR. You may see company employees in jeans, sports jackets or £200 T-shirts, but you still won't go wrong on a first interview being conservative: jacket and tie for the men, simple blouse and jacket or conservative dress for the women. Also, because some companies may bring you back for three or four interviews, make a note indicating what you wore to each. You might want to wear a different coloured tie or blouse for the next round.

Pay attention to details. If the last time you wore your overcoat was at a protest or rally, be sure that you have removed any vestige of the event. I recall a very bright, attractive university graduate who "blew herself out of the water" with a prestigious consulting firm when, despite her good answers and conservative image, she was rejected because she had brought a handbag covered with buttons showing peace signs and marijuana leaves and was wearing green nail polish. Be smart.

So, you know where you are going, who is going to interview you, how much time you will need to spend at the company office, and what you are going to wear. You have also reviewed your paperwork. Now think about what you want to bring with you to the interview, just in case. An extra copy of your CV? Copies of letters of reference? Your referees' addresses and phone numbers? A copy of a project on which you worked? Your marks, perhaps? Certainly a pen and diary. On the day of the interview you may not need any of them, but you'll have them if you do. Have you something to carry those papers in? Have you a briefcase or a folder which won't be ruined in the rain? A special note for women: avoid carrying these three items: handbag, briefcase and umbrella. Put your money and lipstick — even the umbrella — into the briefcase, so that you will have only one item in your hands when it is time to shake hands with your interviewers.

And everyone should practise that handshake prior to

interviewing. When you meet friends, take their hands and shake them. What you want to avoid is a knuckle breaker or a dead fish. Just offer a good handshake. Grip the hand with the thumb pressed against the back of the other person's hand. Silly again? A good strong handshake leaves a good first impression and a poor one hurts it.

Standard Interview Questions

You are looking good, but now to the harder stuff — preparing for the questions. Accept the fact that you cannot anticipate all of them, but there are some questions which occur frequently and which you can think through in advance. The phrasing may vary, but the intent or essence is the same. The interviewer is after the same type of information:

"What is your greatest strength?"

"What is your greatest weakness?"

"Where do you see yourself in five years?"

"What's the biggest challenge you've had? How did you meet it?"

"What is the greatest problem facing the world? Our industry? What recommendations do you have?"

"What was the last film/book you saw/read?"

"Why did you leave your last job?"

Use the company's application as a reference. Reread your copy. What questions were asked? How did you answer them? During the interview you may be asked to expand on any one or all of them: "You indicated on your application that _____. Would you explain what you meant by _____?" Be ready to explain and have an example at hand.

What's your greatest strength?

Let's look at the list: What's your "greatest strength" is no longer a problem. You have your self-inventory, so just look in the plus column. Are you a good problem-solver? Are you patient? Determined? Thorough? A good listener? Analytical? Organised? Dependable? Sensitive? Empathetic? Understanding? Efficient? Knowledgeable in word processing? A team player? A quick learner? Be ready to name a strength and be ready to support it with examples from your experiences in school, at work or in your leisure time. This is not the time to be bashful. There is competition out there!

What about weaknesses?

Frankly, the choices that we overheard in Brendan's conversation are not great. This is not a time for true confessions. Yes, be honest but be sensible, too. In other words, select a genuine weakness and couch it in realistic terms, not self-denigrating ones. Maybe you are "more reflective than you should be". Perhaps you "get impatient with yourself for not meeting your own standards". Sometimes you "take on too much work", because you know that you "should say no and don't". Sometimes you are "too direct". Once again, have an anecdote ready or an example of how you are trying to modify the behaviour. Certainly your weakness is not that you're "always late", you "don't get on with people" or that you "cannot handle numbers" or you are "easily intimidated" or that you are "shy". One of the best answers to "What's your greatest weakness?" was "Chocolate!" Sadly, it's been used, so find another.

Why are you applying? Why should we hire you?

Again, this is not a time to be self-effacing. So why *are* you applying? It is a given that you want or need a job or a change, but the answer should be about the position and the company and what you can bring to both that makes you an asset. You are applying because styling hair is what you have wanted to do. Give examples. You are applying because during school, you learned to work in teams. Give examples. You are applying because you bring X skills for which this company is looking. Give examples. If there is one key recommendation about initial interviewing, it is that you bear in mind what you can do for the company, *not* what they can do for you. Save your own needs for the salary and benefit negotiating.

What are your long-term career goals? Where do you see yourself in five years?

The answers to those questions should be honest and should relate to the organisation. It is unwise to indicate that you plan to open your own business or that you want to retire to work on your novel or to save up and sail to New Zealand. Recruiting and interviewing are expensive, and companies invest money in their employees. They expect to train you formally and informally, so they need reassurance that you are planning to stay, not to walk out.

For most of us, the answer to where we see ourselves in five years is that we don't know; we can't know. You need an answer, though, so think about what you want to learn, the new challenges or increased responsibility that you would like to have. This is not the time to be specific. Don't say that you want to be Vice-president of Tremendo or Head of Personnel or in a corner office overlooking your Merc parked in the car park below. You may actually threaten your interviewer with such answers, so talk about the job functions you would like to grow into within the field or industry.

If the company makes widgets, avoid announcing that you want to run a competing widget company or to be a ballet dancer. You would be amazed at how many people in interviews say just that sort of thing. Remember there is "letting it all hang out", and there is "smart". In fact, if you get the job and if you are successful at what you do and are enjoying it, you may no longer dream of creating your own widgets or sailing to New Zealand.

What's the biggest challenge you've had? What's the greatest problem facing the world, the industry today?

Frankly, whether you pick pollution, war, disease, technology or something else, the specific choice usually doesn't matter. There is no right or wrong answer to such questions. Each one is a problem, large or small, and typically the interviewer will be looking for how you present your argument and the process by which you problem-solve. Do you do everything yourself? Do you share ideas? Do you listen? Are you tyrannical? Do you shoot from the hip? Are you indecisive? Are you politically naïve? Think about Tremendo itself or the industry. Do you see a problem facing it? Prepare for the question. You are not there because you have all the answers; you are there to articulate and to present a reasonable position rationally. You will have to do that on the job all the time.

What was the last book you read? What was the last film that you saw?

Shame on you if you are not ready for these. Among the things that most people write under "interests" in their CVs is that they like sports, or aerobics, reading, going to films, playing soccer, travelling. Please, when you review your CV, examine the list that you wrote and be ready if asked to discuss any items that you wrote. For example, if you said you like reading, then the inter-viewer will expect you to be reading something cur-rently. If you like to travel, be ready to say where you have been. If you like films, be sure that you have seen one recently that you can talk about. "That's obvious," you say. But people often write on their CVs that they like to read but when asked at an interview, "What have you read?" they draw a blank. No one says your choice has to be *Business & Finance* or Philip Kotler; it can be *The Firm* or Michael Crichton's latest. Just be ready to talk about it.

Why did you leave your last job?

The answer to this question is probably one of the most revealing that you will give. Based on your response, the interviewer can anticipate why you might leave the company if they were to employ you. You do *not* want to answer, "I didn't get on with the boss" or "Well, I hated the pressure" or "I was always late" or "I was bored" or "I got a better offer" or "They didn't pay me enough". Think about it. You are literally hinting at what may cause you to leave the new position. Your answers can be interpreted to suggest that you don't get on with people or that you need a calm environment or that you are easily seduced by money or that you are impertinent or resentful. You must be careful how you phrase the answer to this question. If the truth is that you were bored, think about why and turn the answer around. What do you need to keep you going? Challenge? Something new to learn? Consider using positive reasons for leaving rather than negative ones. In other words, it was not that you felt claustrophobic in the three-person company; you wanted the opportunity to work in a larger one. It was not that no one could make a decision; you prefer a more structured environment. And you certainly didn't hate the boss!

To prepare, it is helpful to arrange some mock interviews. Your friend can help you practise. Find 30 minutes and play it out from opening handshake to closing farewells. If you can, record it on a camcorder or audio cassette and play it back. If you practise, you'll become more comfortable and better able to handle the stress of the actual interview.

In addition to preparing for some of the questions you may be asked, think about some of the ones that you want to ask your prospective employer. Typically, at the end the interviewer will say, "Have you any questions for us (or for me)?" Do have some. Ideally, some questions may arise for you in the course of the interview, so ask those. Generally your own questions at this point should be about the job, about the company, about the nature of your responsibilities, the training, the support systems and about the hiring process. A first interview is usually too soon to raise issues of salary and benefits.

In fact, you should have your own questions because interviewing is a two-way process. As they are interviewing you, you are interviewing them. Do you really want the kind of work that they have to offer? Of course, in a tough market you may be willing to accept any position, but a job is 40, 50, 60, 70 hours a week of your life. Even if you leave the office or plant at 4.30 or 5 p.m. you take the work or the work environment home with you. Whom you work with, the ability to get the job done, the duties you have affect your satisfaction. If what you are doing or whom you are working with makes you angry, frustrated, unhappy or disappointed, you are not going to be an effective, productive employee.

So, early on in the interview process you want to know whether the job or the working environment would make you miserable. Therefore, ask questions that will enable you to gain insight into the structure of the organisation, into what the company values are and how they treat their employees. Consider questions like:

"Why is the position open?"

"To whom would I report?"

"How do you train people?"

"Would you outline some of the additional responsibilities?"

"What is your appraisal system?"

"What is the hiring process?"

"Do you plan to enter the _____ market?"

"What are the lines of communication?"

"Will I be responsible for my own budget?"

One last suggestion before your interview: get a good night's sleep and have breakfast or lunch (no garlic) so that your stomach doesn't rumble or your energy level flag in the middle of the interview. To do well, you need to prepare in advance to have your wits about you on the day.

Chapter 7

TRYING TO GET THE OFFER: THE INTERVIEW

The interview day has arrived. You are looking good, you are feeling fine, but you are nervous; you have made the right travel arrangements and arrived on time at the appointed place, briefcase or folder in hand. Arrive a few minutes early. You will have a chance to take a deep breath, to use the loo, to straighten your tie or collar, to comb your windblown hair or to clean the mud off your shoes.

When you reach your destination, more than likely the first person you will meet is a secretary or receptionist. Make a good impression. Smile, be gracious, introduce yourself and indicate with whom you have the appointment. Never forget that receptionists and secretaries are in the front line; they know everyone in the company, and they invariably convey their impressions and thoughts about the people they meet to the people they work for. If you are personable and polite, that information will get back to the right people, in the same way that coldness or bad manners will. Understand that walking in the door is part of the interview process, as is any other contact that you may have with the company.

While you are waiting and are perusing a company brochure or skimming through a magazine or newspaper, look and listen to what is happening around you.

Notice what is going on in the office. Notice the looks on faces and how people are working. Do you see people reading the newspapers or drinking coffee? Do you see people working and smiling? Do you sense tension? Remember you are being interviewed to work there. Does it feel right? Is there a collection of today's papers, or is there only a dog-eared four-month old copy of *The Economist* for you to read? Is the phone ringing off the hook or is it quiet? How are people dressed? All men? What ages? How are you treated while you are waiting? Like number 63 or like a person? If you are made to wait a long time, does someone explain to you that there is a delay, or are you ignored and left wondering what has happened? Are the offices barren? What do the desks look like? Although you may not be able to interpret what all this information means, the organisation is making an impression on you, for good or bad, and you are forming your own impression of it.

In time, you will either be escorted into or directed to the room where you will be interviewed. Remember, this is not a meeting with the headmaster or school principal. You were not caught smoking in the bathroom. This is a meeting between two professionals, both of whom want to like each other. The company wants the right person as much as you want the right job, so smile through your anxiety and be the charming, amiable self that you know you can be, not a scared, bold child waiting to be scolded.

Ah, the handshake — no problem. Now, you will be offered a chair. Remember your manners: do not sit until invited to, but, if you are not invited to, ask if you may. Like the impressions you got in the waiting area, the seating arrangement in the room can be equally revealing. Are you being interviewed across a desk or asked to sit beside it? Is the office large, and are you asked to sit on a sofa while the interviewer joins you? Or are you sitting across a conference room or board-room table? Are you sunk deep in a chair or perched on a stool? Comfortable? Do your legs reach the floor? Quickly scan the room. Pictures? Paper? Disorder? Neatness? Awards? Prizes? Stacks of files or computer paper? Everything you see will affect your judgment of the company and will help you decide whether or not this is a place you want to work.

There are different kinds of interviews and inter-viewers. Some are highly trained in the process. Such interviewers might have carefully prepared questions which are asked of every candidate in order to demon-strate equity in hiring. You will encounter other inter-viewers who may have had less opportunity or training in interviewing, so their questions may be more casual or even downright inappropriate. Although your per-sonal life is no one's business but your own, some inter-viewers, in an effort to be chatty, may pry. You always have the option graciously to decline to answer ques-tions you believe to be intrusive.

Most interviews are designed to relax you in the first minute or two. Interviewers fully understand that the next 30 minutes or so are important to you, so they open the session by breaking the ice with small talk, such as whether or not you had any difficulty finding the office. Questions like those are designed to get you talk-ing and to put you at your ease.

Once the small talk is over, however, there are sev-eral possibilities. One is the stress interview. Here the interviewers show no warmth and pose one difficult question after another, frequently asking how you would solve this or that kind of problem. And when you have given your answer, the interviewer will probe with: "Why?" "When?" "But, what if...?" These kinds of interviews are certainly not comfortable, but sometimes they are less dangerous than the approach used by the interviewer who sits beside you on the sofa and chats. In the former, you may be on guard, while in the latter, you may relax too much. Frequently, candidates do not realise that they are being scrutinised and they become so at ease with the interviewer that all their foibles, idiosyncrasies and private expectations of opening their own business in two years come tumbling out.

Most interviews, though, are a combination of standard questions about your strengths, weaknesses, long-term plans, problem-solving, etc., followed by some probing general questions or industry-specific ones. When you answer, don't go on at great length. Answer the question, give an example or rationale and then wait for the next one. When you answer, maintain eye contact with the interviewer. If there are several interviewers, then answer everyone, not just the person who posed the question. Since we are mentioning non-verbal language, watch your posture. In other words, behave as if you are eager to get the job. Sit up and forward in the chair and don't slouch. Sure, it's hard if you are asked to sit in a deep overstuffed sofa. There are horror stories of people who are asked to sit in a chair in which the front two legs are shorter than the back two. Try to maintain your decorum while sliding off the seat!

Which brings up another point. Should you accept the coffee, tea or cigarette when it is offered? The answer is, it is entirely up to you. If you want a cup of tea or coffee or a cigarette, have one. Games used to be played with cigarette smokers; the interviewers would

offer the candidate a cigarette and then have no ashtrays
in sight. What would the candidate do with the match or
ashes? Some would hold out one hand and catch the
dropping ash, others would use the bin and some,
wisely, would ask for an ashtray. Remember you are not
being naughty; you and your interviewer are adults
talking, so if you have a problem — sliding off the chair,
no ashtray, a dry mouth — ask for assistance. On the
job, if you have a problem that you cannot solve yourself, what would you do? Ask for help, of course! By
the way, the company is also appraising your social
graces, which is why some interviews are held over
lunch. Can you handle yourself at a client lunch? Be
cautious about your alcohol consumption and avoid
ordering sloppy food. Skip the spaghetti bolognese,
much as you may love it!

So be enthusiastic, smile, maintain eye contact, and
keep the employer in mind. Although for you the goal
may be a job, a pay cheque, a possible career, think
about what's in it for the company. The interviewers
want to know if you will fit into their culture. They are
seeking to determine not only what you know, but also
how willing or able you are to learn or to be flexible.
They are assessing your honesty and your commitment.
For an organisation, a new employee is expensive in
terms of salary and benefits and because of the costs of
both formal and informal training. No matter how much
you already know, there is still time required from
others to assist in your development. So keep the company's needs foremost: how will your talents benefit
them? Again, what is in it for them?

Earlier, you were reminded that the interview is not a
disciplinary hearing, so don't treat it as such. Display
your charm, your sense of humour — carefully, of

course. Avoid remarks about sex, religion and politics. Suppose you are thrown a tough question, a "How would you handle _____?" or "What would you do if_____?" Say, "That is a difficult question, I want to think about it." Organisations may be distrustful of people who have all the answers all the time. You are hired to think, so be reflective. Rarely are there right and wrong answers in interviews; it is how you answer and how you handle yourself under the pressure of the situation that is im-portant. The interviewers are well aware that this is an important meeting for you, so don't worry about being nervous.

Answer the questions honestly and sensibly with the company's interests in mind. Keep your objective in mind, too — an offer or a second interview — and let the interviewers know how much you want to work for their company. Sure, they are aware that you are applying elsewhere; you have to be. But reinforce the idea that this is the job that you want. Some candidates in their innocence will say that this position is a second choice or that they "really would prefer to work in the aviation industry", while they are sitting in the office of a retailer. Be smart. If you are asked whether you are applying elsewhere, tell the truth but don't give specific names. And speaking of giving names, just as you did on your CV, observe confidentiality. If you are asked to discuss a confidential project, refer to the nature of the industry, not the specific company. As in the case of your CV, your interviewers are learning how confidential you will be when and if you come to work for them.

At this time, you may be asked to provide the name of your referees, if you have not already done so, which is why you have their names, addresses and phone numbers with you. You will now know what the next step in

the hiring process is: second interview, meeting with
another manager, assessment tests. Let the interviewers
know that you want the job. Thank them. Then say
good-bye and thank the receptionist or secretary on the
way out. Then take a deep breath.

Chapter 8

AFTER THE INTERVIEW

Unless you are an exceptional human being, by the time you have shaken hands with the interviewer(s) and thanked the receptionist, you will be kicking yourself about your inadequate responses or the brilliant point that you forgot to make. You will say things like, "How could I be so stupid!", "Why didn't I remember to tell them about the time I _____?", "Darn, I forgot to mention my _____". This is normal. It is exactly what you've done when you walked out after an exam. "Oh, I forgot", "Why didn't I _____?" Worse yet, you start comparing your answers with those of other people. How did you answer? *Their* responses, of course, are always better than yours!

It is human to feel that way, but after a few minutes, postmortems are self-defeating. If you genuinely forgot to include something, just remember to say it the next time, but don't expend a great deal of energy after your interview on "what if"s and "oh darn"s. You have work to do, including jotting down the questions. You will encounter some of them again or variations on them, and you will want to think through your answers.

If the interviewer asked for your referees' names or for copies of letters of reference, then you had better find a telephone quickly to let each referee know that you were interviewed by Tremendo, plc, and that Mr O'Brien may be phoning. To assist your referee, describe the position and the company's requirements.

That way, the referees will be better able to highlight specific qualities of yours that are suited to the position.

Even if the interviewers did not request the names of your referees, you have work to do. Although again there are two schools of thought about this, most people support the notion that a follow-up letter to an interviewer is important, so you need to draft one. Write to thank Mr O'Brien for the time he gave you and then briefly underline how your particular skills would be useful on the job as you now know it, based on the interview. Reinforce your enthusiasm for the position and mention that point you forgot during the interview. The argument for such a letter is basically that it cannot hurt and may very well help. It is a gracious gesture and tells the employer you want the position.

Now, rather than stewing for the next two weeks wondering whether or not you will get the offer, keep moving on your job hunt, perhaps not on the day of the interview because interviews are stressful and you will probably feel emotionally drained. But the next day, check the papers, or make a phone call. In other words, do something else to put your name forward again, because if you wait for the phone call to come from Tremendo, it may be another two weeks and, despite your best efforts, the answer may be "no". In the interim you will have to consider using your network again. Perhaps you will let someone know that you were interviewed by Tremendo, and that you want the job — if you do. Perhaps that contact can lobby for you by putting in a good word. Be careful, though. Don't use too much pressure. It may backfire. In any event, get your CV and name out for another position while you are waiting to hear. Be proactive!

Time goes by. The phone rings or the letter comes.

Great news. You are invited back for testing or for a second interview or to meet someone else. Prepare just as you did before: get more information on the company, from the library, from friends, from the press. Talk to someone in your evolving network who knows the industry. In other words, learn. Reread your CV. Review the questions that you were already asked. Recall your answers.

If you are invited back for testing, get some rest and don't try to outmanoeuvre personality or psychological tests by manipulating your responses. For example, if you try to select responses that may present you as an outdoor type when you are not, or an introvert when you are the opposite, or action-oriented when you are reflective, you are not going to be happy. Answer truthfully. You also don't know what results the company is looking for when the test is scored. It is possible that a certain response profile has been successful for them in the past; it is also possible that they are looking for profiles different from those of current employees. They may be assessing a new test. In essence, the test may only be a small part of the whole hiring process. It may be another hurdle. My advice: get some rest and be yourself.

Suppose you are invited back, not for testing, but to meet the person or persons for whom or with whom you will be working. Plan to be even more direct with them about the nature of the job and its responsibilities. This is another opportunity for you to interview them, as much as it is a chance for them to interview you. You are the one who is going to do the job, so ask questions and find out if you will be able to do it. Find out about the support system. What technology is available? What training? Is there clerical or secretarial support? Are you it? Is there a budget? How much? Who administers it? Who develops it? Who gives approval for what? Is everything done in committee or have you some autonomy? What are the resources? The working styles? The goals and the expectations for you? The department? The company? What are the problems? What's the relationship with head office? It is your turn to probe. Don't be bashful. You are going to have to live with the position. Remember, there are few jobs that you can forget about at the end of the day or at the end of the shift, so be sure this is the one that you want to commit to and that this is an environment in which you can work.

Behave as you did in your previous interview: be prudent, be enthusiastic and support your arguments with evidence. And if you're asked about in-company problems, be wary of offering instant solutions to problems with which the organisation may have been wrestling for some time. Unless you have time to assess the situation, you don't know; however, let the interviewers know how you've tackled similar problems or what methods you prefer to use to solve problems in general. And as you did before, express your interest in the position. In addition, terms and condition of employment will arise now. Begin to learn about evaluation processes, how excellence is rewarded, and what your expenses are and what is underwritten by the organisation.

Following the interview, if you have not let your referee know that you are a finalist, do so now! But brace yourself. At any point during the application and interview process, you may be knocked out — after the application, after the first, second or even third interview. You could be one of two, and yet the other candidate could get the job. You'll be hurt, of course, and the closer you are to getting it, the more it will hurt. You'll be angry and disgusted. It is disappointing and it is infuriating. Coming to terms with those feelings is important. You may swear, sulk, resign yourself, bemoan your fate, blame others, decide that you are a loser, call the whole process unfair. In sports, aren't we tempted to blame the ref, the coach, the field, the weather, a stomach virus? But try not to dwell on your loss too long. You didn't make the sale, and it is disappointing, but it is also time to get on with your life. In this instance, try again.

Earlier we said that rejection isn't personal. Not being selected is not always about you, your personality, your hair colour, the choice of suit that you wore, or whether or not you accepted the coffee. You can't know what went on in the company after the interview, the corporate decision-making that occurred. You can't know who else was interviewed, what particular talents they may have offered. You can't know that the company may have decided to balance the department by bringing in a young man with a college degree or a young woman from Galway with two years' experience in the field. You can't know that they have decided that the nature of the position, in fact, may be too repetitive for you; you can't know that they decided to move someone internally and to advertise for a less responsible position or that they decided to redesign the position or to readvertise it. In other words, there are variables which have nothing to do with you, so don't take what may appear to be a rejection personally.

Be the consummate professional if you lost, painful as it may be. Write a letter thanking the company for their time and letting your interviewer know that you

still want to work for the company and that you hope
you will be considered for another position in the future.
Athletes and other competitors come in second and
third and fourth all the time, and they live with it. The
key is to come to terms with your feelings quickly and
to learn from the experience. Certainly there is no harm
in phoning your interviewers and asking for feedback.
They may or may not give it because in a litigious age,
interviewers are careful about what reasons they give
you for not hiring you. You may hear only that "it was a
difficult decision". Emotionally it is important that you
"feel the pain" and get on with it. And "getting on with
it" means putting out more feelers. The reality is that
sometimes not getting the position is for the better. In
fact, the company or the position might stifle you, and
although you were interviewing well, the organisation
may be too big or too small, or too structured or too
unstructured. The communication systems may be
weak. The supervisor may be a tyrant. Think about it.
All along you may have been getting signals that the
organisation was not the right environment for you.
Bottom-line: if the result of the interview is "no", reflect
on what you have learned, and keep applying.

Sometimes, of course, it is going to be "yes". Most
of us are ready for "no", but what if you are made an
offer? Are you ready for "yes"? Beware of being so
delighted at the outcome that you forget that this is
business, so be ready to negotiate for a starting date and
money or anything else that you want or need.

Besides the financial package, starting date is important. Suppose the company wants you to begin working
in a week? If you are employed or are committed elsewhere, you may have obligations to your former employer, clients or colleagues, or you may have projects

which need to be wrapped up, explained or transferred. Therefore, negotiate for a starting date whether it is in one, two or four weeks. Allow yourself enough time so that you can leave your current position without any rancour or stress. Your former employer might very well be a referee for you in the future. In addition, your new boss should respect your sense of responsibility, because he or she knows that should you leave this new position sometime in the future, you are likely to do so with the same sense of loyalty and thoughtfulness. In other words, put your starting date needs on the table. Professional commitment might not be the only reason for negotiating a starting date; you may have surgery planned or a holiday or a class scheduled. Let the new organisation know. Most companies are willing to work around personal plans or problems, but put them on the table at the outset as well.

In the later interviews or now, when an offer of the position is being made, your remuneration package will come up for discussion. Most of us are not independently wealthy, nor do we work for love. We expect to be paid fairly for our efforts. So, as was suggested earlier, calculate the amount you need to live on and what you would reasonably like to have. You will probably settle for a salary somewhere in between. The amount of your starting salary, however, may govern all future increases. For example, if you start at £8,000 and raises are annual and are based on a percentage, hypothetically 3 per cent, then next year you will earn £8,240. If, however, you start at £8,500, and get a 3 per cent raise, then your salary becomes £8,755, so it is important to set a figure that is realistic and negotiable.

Enquire about the benefits: sick pay, personal days, vacation leave, health plans, dental, optical, group discounts. Are there bonuses? How are they calculated? Are they based on merit? Is there profit-sharing? What about pension schemes? Are there discounts on products? Also include in your thinking the "perks", such as a company canteen with prices so low that you can save £5 a day on lunches. Is there a health club? Will you be wearing a uniform or will you have to invest in new clothing? Will you have to relocate or rent a flat? Are you eligible for overtime?

In other words, tot up all of your costs and then be ready with a realistic figure, because you may be asked what you want, or you may be told what the company is prepared to offer. Let them know what you want or need, and negotiate. For example, if you want £16,000 and they offer only £15,000 but are willing to pay for additional courses, that may be acceptable to you. If however, they offer only £14,000 to start, negotiate a review in three months.

Also find out what kind of contract you are being offered — three months, six months, one year, two years? Who evaluates you? How often? Are you tied into union contracts? Are vacations scheduled by seniority? Does the company close down for a month? Who gets company cars? Can you have access to one if you need it? How is transportation handled? How are out-of-pocket expenses handled? Is there an expense account? Is there a company credit card? Are you reimbursed? How soon?

The point here is that you must beware of being so excited at receiving an offer that you forget to absorb the details. If you do, you risk being angry with yourself in three months for not having asked at the negotiation stage. At the same time, you may decide that getting into an organisation which offers you a career or opportunity may be far more important than the job title, the corner office or the company canteen. Keep your demands in perspective.

However, let us introduce another scenario. Suppose you were just made an offer by Tremendo, plc, and Microtech is asking you to come back for a second interview next week. What do you do? If you want to work at Tremendo, it's easy. Say "Yes" to them and "No, thank you" to Microtech. However, if you want to see how both positions evolve because they are both intriguing, then you are going to have to play for time, but fairly. You may want to tell Microtech that you have another offer, but that you are interested in them as well. You may try to have the date of the interview moved forward because you want to give an answer to Tremendo. Microtech may be impressed with your candour and agree to move the date.

Let's make matters worse: maybe they can't move the date, because the interviewer is away. Thus, you could find yourself in the awkward position of being fearful of losing the offer from Tremendo, but wanting to see what happens with Microtech. It is a risk that you may want to take. You could tell Tremendo that you are a finalist with another organisation where there is a potential for more responsibility or more money. Therefore, as much as you welcome the opportunity of working for them, you want to follow up on the other one. You can't control their response; the interviewers at Tremendo may put you under pressure, or they may give you a deadline: "We need to know in one week." In fact, you may have to decide immediately and withdraw from one or from the other. Old sayings like "A bird in the hand" may cross your mind, cancelled out by "Nothing ventured, nothing gained". In other words, it is a tough call, and you will have to weigh the pros and cons as well as Tremendo's willingness to wait. You are probably laughing at this scenario, because you don't believe it, but it happens. Like buses, job offers come in herds.

Chapter 9

IT AIN'T OVER YET

Congratulations! You have received an offer that meets your requirements, a job that you are looking forward to and a starting date that meets your needs and the company's. Enjoy the honeymoon!

As you settle in behind your new desk, remember that jobs are no longer for life. More than likely, you will have more than one move during your career, within the same industry or in another, or you may find yourself working in different countries. Furthermore, personal circumstances may cause you to move. With an increasing number of couples where both partners have careers, change is inevitable, so, strange as it sounds, the minute you get your new job update your CV. In fact, always keep your CV current. Don't forget to add the degree that you have just been awarded or to add in the summer project that was just completed. Add accomplishments. One reason for doing this is that sometimes for reasons other than job-changing purposes you are asked for a copy of your CV. Your organisation may be putting your name forward, or you might be speaking at a conference.

Suppose, though, that you already have a job but that you are looking for another one. A number of sensitive issues are involved here. You are aware that there are those bosses who will resent your leaving their employment. Some other bosses will understand and will even help you look for a new position, particularly if they realise that there are either personal or work-related circumstances which are affecting you, such as an un-realistic commute, an ailing family member or the realisation that the company cannot offer you more challenge, growth or money, that you have gone as far as you can go. You have given them service and com-mitment, but there may be no future for you at the company.

Enlightened supervisors support your efforts and may ask how your search is progressing or tell you if they hear of something, or even put your name forward. In exchange, however, they will want to be kept informed of your progress in the event that they need to replace you. On the other end of the continuum, there are supervisors who will perceive your wanting to leave as disloyalty. "How dare you desert the ship, you rat!" they'll think, or say. Such individuals may have power needs which suggest that only they, not you, may con-trol your destiny. As a candidate for a position, you are going to have to make an educated guess about whether or not to tell your current employer that you are in the job market. Certainly, there is no point in telling anyone anything until you are a serious candidate, and by seri-ous candidate is meant someone who is being called back, someone who is a finalist. Your employer does not need to know every time your CV has gone out, unless you feel that the work community is so small that he or she will know and will be angered by your failure to communicate your intentions.

Prospective employers know that this dilemma is a common one with job candidates, which is why applica-tions frequently ask the question: "May we contact your current employer?" Be frank in the interview and indi-cate that you do or do not want them to make contact at the present time. When you know the process is down to the wire, then it is time to let your current employer know. He or she is, in fact, a key reference, unless there are unusual circumstances why they should or should not be. Tell your current employer that you are a finalist and ask for their support. Be ready to explain why you are applying. Be ready, too, for a range of reactions from "Wonderful" to "How could you!"

You have an obligation to keep your supervisor informed because should you receive an offer you may have to be replaced and, therefore, time will be needed to recruit, interview, hire and train your replacement. Your supervisor will expect a realistic time frame — and "realistic" is not 3–6 months. You yourself have a new job to learn, so watch your generosity of spirit when you write a letter of resignation. The shorter, the better. Once you have agreed a starting date with your new employer, bear in mind the impact of your departure on your current one. Then write a letter which reads something like this:

Dear Mr Green,

Effective 30 June 199x I am resigning my position as _____. My _____ years working for you have provided me with _____, and I thank you for the opportunity of _____.

Yours sincerely,

In other words, leave officially, politely, thoughtfully and gracefully.

There is another scenario fraught with emotion, and

which is related to your being promoted within the company. Say a job is posted, you apply, are interviewed and get it. Most likely some of your colleagues will have applied as well and been rejected. Remember the words we used earlier to describe your own feelings of rejection: "angry", "jealous", "frustrated" and "disappointed". That is what they may be feeling. You, however, are euphoric. The wise supervisor will talk to the people who were turned down, but you may want to clear the air as well by being empathetic, by making them aware that you know how they feel and that you want to work together. They will still be hurt, but empathy goes a long way to easing that pain.

Again, a point that cannot be repeated enough: do not forget your referees! Do not forget your network! It is time to tell people that you are grateful to them for what they have done for you. And they will be interested in knowing how your career is developing. Call your referees. Thank them and stay in touch. Two years down the road, you may need them again, or they may need you in your new capacity!

Selling yourself is a competitive business. Believe in yourself and understand the market. It's hard work. It involves phoning, writing, and rewriting and talking and being subject to emotions like joy, rejection, disappointment and jealousy. But it is a wonderful feeling to have worked hard and won and to have a job where you have an opportunity to learn and grow and to help an organisation grow, too. In your new position don't forget that there are others who are now sitting over coffee talking to their friends, feeling frustrated or downcast. So offer a hand. Be part of their network, give advice, help with mock interviews. Teach them some of the lessons that you have learned.